JOURNEY TO EMMAUS

To Roni and Julian Oswald

DAVID FORRESTER

Journey to Emmaus

A Retreat to do at Home

ST PAULS

Cover design by Richard Budd of Lionheart Graphics Ltd.

ST PAULS Publishing
187 Battersea Bridge Road, London SW11 3AS, UK
www.stpaulspublishing.com

Copyright © ST PAULS 2009
ISBN 978-0-85439-768-6

A catalogue record is available for this book from the British Library.

Set by Tukan DTP, Stubbington, Fareham, UK
Printed and bound in Great Britain by Athenaeum Press Ltd,
Gateshead, Tyne & Wear, UK

ST PAULS is an activity of the priests and brothers
of the Society of St Paul who proclaim the Gospel
through the media of social communication

Contents

Introduction

Some time ago I was invited to give a retreat to the Benedictine monks of St Andrew's Abbey, at Valyermo, in the Mohave Desert in Southern California. The theme of the retreat first came to mind when I was considering the behaviour of the two disciples who were journeying on the Road to Emmaus, (Lk 24:13-35), after the resurrection of Jesus. (The full account of the Road to Emmaus story can be found in the Appendix.)

I had always wondered what it was that prevented the disciples from recognising Jesus, what caused their hearts to 'burn' within them as they talked with him, and how they finally recognised him at the 'breaking of bread'. My aim in the retreat was to consider these questions, but more especially to ask what prevents each of us from recognising Christ on our particular Road to Emmaus, our path through life, as well as what we can do about it.

Latterly I decided to make my talks to the monks the basis of a retreat for ordinary men and women in their homes. For one reason or another, such as family commitments, work pressures and even costs, many people, priests as well as lay people, are unable to go away to a monastery or retreat centre for the purpose of making a retreat. On the other hand, they might more easily be able to set aside thirty minutes or so each day and, during that time, quietly absorb the contents of one chapter at a time.

No retreat is worthwhile however unless the one leading it practises what he or she preaches. Effective retreat givers are those who place themselves and all their endeavours in the hands of God, which is no mean task. Rather like the painter of an icon who prays before, during and after taking up his tools, making his creative efforts a shared one with God, a retreat giver should seek to become a total instrument in the hands of the Creator of all. Unless he or she does so and thereby never forgets the Psalmist's words "*Non nobis Domine*", "Not to us but to the Lord give the glory", he or she will fail the participants, no matter the brilliance of his or her words and expositions.

Throughout the retreat with the monks at St Andrew's Abbey I was additionally always highly conscious of being in a desert, indeed one could not forget it. The arid landscape, the heat and the constant need to seek the shade were ever present factors in the Mohave Desert. One cannot live for long in a desert without it affecting one's outlook. As was shown in the life of Christ himself and those of the Desert Fathers of the early church, the desert can spiritually be a place of immense intensity, both in terms of trial and temptation. But the absence of worldly distractions can also enable one to get things and issues in perspective and hopefully acquire a measure of wisdom.

For those however who are unable to withdraw into such a place as a desert to make their retreat, it is decidedly a good idea to find a favourite place in their home or garden, if they have one, where they can sit quietly, read one chapter at a time, reflect on it, and conclude their thirty minutes or so with a prayer. At the end of each chapter therefore points for reflection are offered, Scriptural readings are highlighted, and practical ways are suggested in which a person might apply the contents of each chapter to his or her daily life. Additionally at the end of the book is a list of books for possible further reading for those interested. It is also suggested that the account of the experience of the two disciples of Jesus walking on the Road to Emmaus, located in the Appendix, should either be read first, or even better, consulted throughout this Retreat being made at home.

Today the need for the Christian every now and then to make a Retreat, though not necessarily literally in a desert, is more necessary than ever. Writing recently of how modern life can narrow and restrict our vision of reality, the author Frances Young says,

"Modernity has had the effect of crippling our attention so that only this world counts. The 'Quest for the Historical Jesus' has focused on precisely what happened during his life as a historical person, and struggles with narratives, such as the transfiguration or the resurrection, which raise questions beyond those historical parameters. In the modern mind-set heaven has been brought to earth. We expect utopia now: if only we can find the right formula, everything can be put to rights... Risk is eliminated by health and safety legislation and people rush to litigation if anything goes wrong. Life has been extended for many of us beyond the biblical three score years and ten... The majority even of those who have church funerals have no hope beyond this world. So conditions here are now all important. This deeply affects the churches, which are now afraid of the jibe, 'pie in the sky when you die'. Prayer is focused on what happens in the new media, everyone longs for peace now, and so on… All of this breeds unrealism and anxiety about the human condition."

(*Brokenness and Blessing.*
Towards a Biblical Spirituality)

I hope therefore that this attempt to provide a retreat for people in their homes will assist men and women of all ages and backgrounds to obtain a measure of both realism and hope in their lives, as well as enable them to deepen their spiritual lives.

Chapter 1

The Different Approaches to God

"Countless numbers are deceived in multiplying prayers. I would rather say five words devoutly with my heart than five thousand which my soul does not relish with affection and understanding."

(Edmund the Martyr)

Virtually everyone agrees that the very familiar story of Jesus meeting two of his followers on the road to Emmaus after his resurrection is an exquisite story (Lk 24:13-35). It contains many of St Luke's favourite themes, such as encounters made by people on a journey, the question of faith, the offering of hospitality and recognition of Jesus in the Eucharist. It has captured the imagination of countless painters down the centuries from Bassano and Caravaggio to Velasquez and Rembrandt, to name just a handful. It also includes other important elements such as the contrast between the doubts expressed by the two men with the faith of the women who had visited Jesus' empty tomb, and the men's eagerness to return to Jerusalem to share with the eleven their experience of meeting Christ, not to mention what the story tells us about the resurrection appearances of Jesus.

This episode however also serves a practical purpose for us today. As we read it, it asks each of us to examine our own interior disposition towards God as we proceed through life. Socrates once said that the unexamined life is not worth living. The story of the two disciples on the road to Emmaus enables us to look at our own lives and examine how each of us can approach and can find God, no matter what our age and situation in life may be, and especially if we are leading busy and stressful lives.

Although all of us are human and members of one kind or other of a community, whether it is our family, our neighbourhood, an institution, a work place, town, village, or country, everyone of us is unique. We each relate with God in our own particular way and not precisely as do our neighbours. This is how it should be, but how frequently do we ask ourselves whether our approach is appropriate for us?

Take for example those of us who use our imagination when we listen to the story of the Road to Emmaus. We might spend time imagining the feelings of the two disciples, who seemingly almost despaired after the death of Jesus on the cross, the nature of the journey they were making, the topography of the terrain through which they were passing, how they greeted their fellow traveller who joined them, and asking ourselves why they didn't recognise him at first.

From our own experience however we know that imagination is a double edged sword. Appropriately used it is a brilliant instrument enabling us to discover beneath the apparent appearance of things, their inner meaning and significance. Out of control, it can take us on to the dark side of things. It can take us over and control our thoughts and appetites and these, in turn, can lead us into temptation, even addiction and sin.

What does one mean by the imagination? A working definition might be that which allows us to see into and beyond the mystery of what happens. Many influential theologians have prized imagination extremely highly, for example Schleiermacher and John Henry Newman, and more recently Karl Rahner, Hans von Balthasar and Bernard Lonergan. Certain writings of these theologians, encouraging us to use our imagination, enable us to attain for example a deeper awareness and experience of the incarnation of Jesus.

According to the journalist and writer Ronald Rolheiser, "We live in a world that's 'mystically tone-deaf'." From the words and writings of Pope Benedict XVl, we know in what ways our Western society is precisely this. Materialistic, consumer ridden, relativistic in its so-called values, divided and violent, with huge gaps between rich and poor and so on. Rightly used the imagination however is a tool to enable us to see beyond this, but it is more than just a mental attribute. It transforms through grace our understanding both of revelation (how God shows himself) and our humanity, the question of who we are. No less a figure than Albert Einstein was of the view that imagination is more important than knowledge.

Formularies and doctrines, vitally important though they are, will never do complete justice to mystery. It is imagination that enables us to see into and beyond the mystery of what happens. As the writer W. Wright, author of *Sacred Heart, Gateway to Heaven,* says,

> "A layered reality is part of the Catholic imagination. To possess this imagination is to dwell in a universe inhabited by unseen

presences – the presence of God, the presence of the saints, the presence of one another. This life transcends the confines of space and time."

Another writer, Daniel O'Leary, further suggests that,

"It takes immense imagination to take the Incarnation literally, to identify God's signature on everything around us, to see God's face behind every face, to discover the Lover-God who comes to us disguised as our lives."

There is also the crucial additional fact that imagination and beauty are related. Both can rescue worship for example from being dull and repetitive and become instead an encounter with God. Both imagination and beauty can provide for our inbuilt need for transcendence and the numinous. A paradoxical way of putting it is, as Picasso once said,

"Art is a lie which makes us realise the truth."

Anyone conversant with such poets as William Wordsworth and others of the Romantic Movement at the end of the eighteenth and early-nineteenth centuries will be aware of their idea that nature and imagination enable us to discover spiritual depths in the world around us. Or as William Blake says,

"To see the world in a grain of sand
And a heaven in a wild flower
Hold infinity in the palm of your hand
And eternity in an hour."

Nevertheless, as a modern writer once said,

> "imagination and beauty are too often obscured
> by the high walls of logic."

Even so, it makes sense from time to time to ponder whether this way of approaching God is the most effective way for each one of us as individuals and as members of a community. In other words, just as the disciples experienced on the Road to Emmaus how "their eyes were (eventually) opened and they recognised Christ," we need to attempt to do the same within our hearts. Depending on our different make up as individuals, which in turn has been moulded and shaped by our background, upbringing, education, environment and so on, there are a variety of ways of recognising Christ in our lives.

For example, for those in the world on the edges of awareness of God's existence, their discovery of him may be limited and found chiefly in their love of such things as beauty in nature, their wonderment at art and music, the insights they obtain from great works of literature and the discoveries of science, their joy at particular achievements they make, and above all from their experiences, both of suffering and great joy, within human relationships. These latter too are usually where we most often experience authentic love.

Here incidentally, Pope Benedict XVI's encyclical *Deus Caritas Est* is particularly pertinent for bringing in the dimension of Christ. After declaring that St Paul's hymn to charity (1 Cor 13:1ff) "must be the Magna Carta of all ecclesial service" he goes on to say,

"Practical activity will always be insufficient, unless it visibly expresses a love for man, a love nourished by an encounter with Christ."

Furthermore, when Benedict writes of sharing in the needs and sufferings of others as a form of love, he significantly adds self-oblation.

"My deep personal sharing," he says, "in the needs and sufferings of others becomes a sharing of my very self with them: if my gift is not to prove a source of humiliation, I must give to others not only something that is my own, but my very self: I must be personally present in my gift."

Many, possibly most explicit Christians, recognising the truth of Jesus' words to the disciple Philip that to have seen me is to have seen the Father, find God simply through their basic and daily experience of prayer, the reception of his presence in the sacraments, their patient adherence to the teachings of the Church, and their attempt to follow Jesus as the Way, the Truth and the Life. Others will follow this path and are then led to meditate on and deepen their understanding of Christ's existence in revelation, especially in the Scriptures, and ponder on his purpose in coming to share our earthly existence, the role of his mother Mary, and the meaning of redemption.

All these methods of discovery, paths, and ways of living follow what is known as the "kataphatic tradition". They are modes of understanding God through affirmation, including our human experiences of being God's sons and daughters, of loving and being loved, of compassion, justice, and mercy which all tell us by way of analogy something about God. But they cannot penetrate to God's essence. They may enable us to approach God, but none of them can adequately mirror the reality we call God. Because of this, other people follow the path of "apophaticism", a way which renounces knowledge gained from evidence, experiences and symbols. Here the presence of God is known neither in human experience nor by use of the imagination but as "unknown."

Of course those called by God to find him and know him in this quite different way – the way of union through what St Paul and others have termed 'opening the Eye of the Heart' – are neither superior nor especially blessed. This apophatic way, is radically different from the usual everyday methods of getting to know God. But then we are talking about a God whose ways are not our ways, whose thoughts are not our thoughts, and who is essentially a God of paradox. This way has a long tradition in both the Eastern and Western churches and has been followed by such as Gregory of Nyssa, the Pseudo-Dionysius, the author of *The Cloud of Unknowing*, Master Eckhart, John of the Cross and many others. Apophaticism thrives on paradox.

In order to find God as completely ineffable, the author of *The Cloud of Unknowing* says that we should place a "cloud of forgetfulness" between ourselves and all creatures (including concepts and images) and enter a cloud of unknowing. He maintains that, in contemplation, God is known in darkness, that is by not knowing him. Or as Master Eckhart says, "Seek God, so as never to find him." In other words, once one seems to have found God, it is not He whom one has found. Finally, for a person with what is called a religious vocation, all these different ways of discovering and relating with God will be played out in a religious community. But then all of us, technically religious or not, are members of some form of community.

The duty of each and every one of us, however, is to discern which method or way of life is appropriate for us as individuals to live out our lives, humbly and with acceptance. This is so whether one is married or single, young or elderly, rich or poor, healthy or sick. No one way is higher than another, since we are all engaged in finding and encountering God at the very core of ourselves. As St Paul says, "There is a variety of gifts but always the same Spirit" (1 Cor 12:4).

Most people probably combine different approaches or use one method or another depending on their circumstances and their mood at the time. Then again, each of us is different from one another and at the same time all of us are as valuable as one another, reminding us, as someone once said, that standing before another human being we should always remove our shoes, because we are standing on holy ground. And it does not matter who he or she is.

At the beginning of her *Dialogue* St Catherine of Siena invites her reader to enter the 'cell of self-knowledge.' There can be no authentic Christian life that is not one of deepening self-knowledge. This is more than a matter of introspection, a looking within, though it will inevitably include some degree of reflection of heart and mind. It also involves the fundamental understanding that I am made by God, made in his image and likeness, and I am made for God. Furthermore this making of who I am in every moment of my being is an act of God's love for me. I am to know myself above all as a creature loved by

God. I am indeed invited to see myself through God's eyes, with his delight. Only then will I also learn how to see others in this way, and myself as a sinner whom God calls to repentance. The twelfth-century Cistercian, St Aelred of Rievaulx, once wrote in *The Mirror of Charity*,

> "The love of God is, so to speak, the soul of the other loves. It lives of itself with perfect fullness, its presence communicates to the others their vital being, its absence brings about their death. That a person may love himself, the love of God is formed in him; that one may love one's neighbour, the capacity of one's heart is enlarged."

We might think that it is due to our experience of being loved by others that we know what it might be for God to love us, but for Aelred it is the conviction that God loves us unconditionally that then enables us to see ourselves in our true light. Similarly, it was after experiencing Jesus' love in listening and talking with them on the Road to Emmaus and, ultimately, by experiencing his breaking of bread with them that the two disciples finally recognised the truth that Jesus had indeed risen from the dead. Hopefully this will be our experience as we spend part of each day in this retreat in our homes.

Hopefully too we may learn how to encounter Jesus in our lives in a variety of ways, and at the same time understand what those things are which often prevent us from recognising him immediately.

Three questions to reflect upon

1. How do we most usually pray?

2. Do we appreciate that prayer may take many different forms, ranging from seeking God's help to being simply quiet in his company?

3. Where do I find it easiest to pray – before the Blessed Sacrament in church, in my home or outdoors walking alone? Wherever it is organise your life to do it regularly.

Suggested Scriptural readings

Read slowly and reflectively the whole of chapter 13 in St Paul's First Letter to the Corinthians on love. Ask yourself whether this is practicably possible for you.

Practical ideas

1. Allot a portion of each day to prayer and persevere with it. Begin by praying at least for ten minutes and gradually increase the time.

2. Pray in the way most suited to you. This may initially take the form of reciting traditional prayers such as the Our Father and Hail Mary, but do not be afraid to experiment. The aim is always to enter into a dialogue with God, which includes listening to him. Remember nothing kills prayer so much as giving up!

Chapter 2

The Place of Humility

"In order to become an instrument in God's hands we must be of no account in our own eyes."
(Angela Merici)

In ordinary language we speak of knowledge as the acquisition and organisation of facts. We regard an educated person as someone who possesses a large and varied body of information and knows how to deploy such knowledge. If such a person is technically and scientifically minded this might include practical skills. If philosophically and theologically minded such a person would be skilled in theorising and speculating. If a painter, a writer, a musician, or an actor then hopefully his or her gifts enable them to communicate with others. If a physician or psychologist such a person might understand how we function and so on.

This education however, is not of itself sufficient to enable us to encounter God at the core of our being. For this we do not need either cleverness or brilliance. This is illustrated in the story of the young Oxford don who, soon after his appointment to a college, is being shown around it by its head. The young man is trying desperately to impress the head of the college with a display of knowledge. After a few minutes the head of the college stops him and says, "There is no need to show me that you are clever. We are all clever here. Try to be kind, that's much more difficult and considerably more rare here."

One is reminded here too of the words of the great Orthodox saint, Seraphim of Sarov (d.1833), to those who came to him for counsel.

> "You cannot be too gentle, or too kind. Shun even to appear harsh in your treatment of each other. Joy, radiant joy, streams from the face of him who gives and kindles joy in the heart of him who receives."

Similarly, to discover God we need more than worldly knowledge. For an encounter with God we first need to appreciate that he is always there inviting us to enter into a relationship with him. On the Road to Emmaus it was Jesus who first approached the two disciples. And, if we accept God's invitation, then at different times we need trust, patience, perseverance, and self-discipline. Above all and at all times we need the courage to follow God as revealed in the person of Christ, or as St Paul tells the Philippians, "In your minds you must be the same as Christ Jesus" (Phil 2:5).

For us this means pursuing the path of *kenosis* or self-emptying, which is linked to purity of heart and humility, illustrated in the famous hymn contained in St Paul's Letter to the Philippians, (Phil 2: 6-11). Indeed, without *kenosis*, we shall find that like the two disciples on the road to Emmaus, something prevents us recognising Jesus.

The hymn found in this second chapter of St Paul's Letter is intended to illustrate Christ's humility and contains guidance for us, just as much as for the people of Philippi. Paul prefaces it with a moving plea, as only he knows how to persuade others.

"If our life in Christ means anything to you, if love can persuade at all, or the Spirit that we have in common, or any tenderness and sympathy…"

He does this in order that the Philippians might be united in love, with a common purpose and mind, the one thing he says that would make him completely happy. In other words, they would then experience real fellowship among themselves resting on a common sharing in the gift of the Spirit (*Koinonein*).

Then he asks that there should be no competition or conceit among them and everyone should be self effacing. He tells them that they should always consider others as better than themselves, think of others' interests before their own and have the same mind as that of Christ. (This is comparable to his statement to the people of Corinth that "In the one Spirit we were all baptized, Jews as well as Greeks, slaves as well as citizens, and one Spirit was given to us all to drink." [1 Cor 12:13]).

The Christ Hymn itself:

Who, though his condition was divine,
Jesus did not consider being like God
something to exploit for selfish gain.
But rather he emptied himself,
adopting the condition of a slave
taking on the likeness of human beings.
And being found in human form,
He lowered himself further still,
Becoming obedient unto death
(even death upon a cross).
Wherefore God has highly exalted him
and graciously bestowed upon him the name

23

that is above every other name,
So that at the name of Jesus
every knee should bend,
in heaven, on earth, and under the earth,
And every tongue confess
that Jesus Christ is Lord
to the glory of God the Father.

The structure of this hymn is debated, but theologically it is divided into two, the lowliness or abasement of Jesus contrasted with his exaltation, culminating in the homage we all should give him. It contains echoes of the Old Testament and was perhaps written originally in Greek or Aramaic. It is possible that Paul learnt it in the late 30s after his conversion.

Whatever the nature of the hymn, its aim was and is to persuade us to become humble and obedient to God. Humility in this context means *self-emptying*. Without this, we cannot come to know God. This is its practical use for us whoever and wherever we are. Other saints besides Paul, such as St Benedict in his *Twelve Degrees of Humility* and St Bernard in his exposition of humility, place a similar emphasis on self-emptying. Both saints clearly base their teaching on an awareness that nothing human is worthwhile unless it involves the 'death' of our self-centred self or as Christ himself said,

> "Truly, truly, I say to you unless the grain of wheat falls into the ground and dies, it remains alone; but if it dies, it bears much fruit…"
>
> (John 12:24)

At the Last Supper when Jesus washed his disciples' feet he gave them a memorable demonstration of the value he placed on humility, just as previously he had been adamant about its importance when they had disputed among themselves as to which of them should be considered the greatest.

> "The greatest among you must behave as if he were the youngest, the leader as if he were the one who serves. For who is the greater: the one at table or the one who serves? The one at table, surely? Yet here am I among you as one who serves!" (Luke 22:26-27)

In recent times Donald Nicholl has echoed this and written of the 'liberation' that comes from the death of the false 'I', the ego. "Japanese Buddhists," he says, "speak of two 'I's: one of them is the 'I' that is susceptible to study by psychology, (and that) strives to satisfy its desires, talks about itself, observes its reactions, displays itself, and is eminently visible. It is known as 'shoga' and has to perish if the other 'I' is to be properly born. This latter, known as 'taiga', refers to the whole human being when that whole human being is entirely taken up in aspiration and prayer."[1]

An insight worth adding to this is found in Jean Vanier's book *Becoming Human*, where the author says that, "The death of the false self, the ego, is more painful in people who have created a strong, imposing, and dominating self. Its death is less painful in those who are weaker or who have never sought to have power."

The fundamental question evoked both by the Pauline hymn and subsequent writers however is to what extent are we as humble as Christ? For without true humility we shall not encounter or recognise Christ on our particular Road to Emmaus or journey through life. In this context one is reminded of the story of the hermit who was able to banish demons. This ability puzzled the Desert Mother, Theodora, who questioned the demons about this.

THEODORA: What drives you away? Is it fasting?
DEMONS: We do not eat or drink.
THEODORA: So is it the hermit's vigils?
DEMONS: We do not sleep.
THEODORA: Is it his separation from the world?
DEMONS: We live in the desert ourselves.
THEODORA: So what is it?
DEMONS: Nothing can overcome us, except humility.

An archbishop in Bolivia

Many years ago an Italian priest was sent by his superiors as a missionary to Bolivia, the poorest country in South America. When he arrived he was greatly shocked by the poverty and primitive conditions in which so many of his parishioners lived.

Some years later he was made an archbishop. By that time however he had adopted a way of life which he continued and still today continues to pursue, even though he now has huge responsibilities and many more people to serve. He shares the life style of his people.

Instead of a large house, he continues to live in a modest building with a tin roof, with only cold running water, (sometimes no water at all), and none of the facilities we usually take for granted. He does not own a car, but travels around his diocese by bus. He wears simple clothes, eats simple food and is available at all times for people in need. He never turns anyone away from his door.

Such is the people's trust in him that he is often called upon to act as an arbiter in disputes affecting their livelihood. Some years ago for example and before recent government legislation, the city's water supply was privatised and sold to a consortium of international companies who immediately doubled or tripled the water rates. In what became known as *La Guerra del Aqua,* the war of water, thousands of citizens demonstrated in the streets, resulting in armed troops being called in, arrests being made, one protester being killed and injuries being inflicted on many others. The crisis was only solved when the archbishop persuaded both the water companies to back down and the protesters to disperse.

The archbishop is also renowned for his personal acts of charity. On one occasion for example, he personally paid for the medical treatment of a young thief set on fire by an angry mob, when caught in the very act of stealing. At the same time as the archbishop rebuked those responsible for inflicting third degree burns on the young man, he also berated the police for not providing adequate security against such criminal acts as theft.

The people love him. Whilst they never forget that he is an archbishop, they are never over-awed or frightened to approach him. They recognise that he cares for them. They see in him the kind of disciple spoken of by Jesus in the Gospel; someone like himself who "came not to be served but to serve".

> "Anyone who wants to be great among you must be your servant, and anyone who wants to be first among you must be your slave."
>
> (Mt 20:26-27)

This is a fundamental requirement of any one wishing to encounter Jesus on his or her particular journey in this life.

Questions for Reflection

1. How do you describe humility and why is it so necessary in our relationship with God?
2. What sort of things do we learn when we are genuinely humble in relation to others?

Scriptural reading

Slowly consider the hymn in Philippians 2 by first reading it again and then following the analysis below.

"His condition (state) was divine" refers to Christ's essential character as Godlike.

"Did not cling" means that Christ did not exploit his exalted status for selfish ends.

"Emptied himself" or *kenosis* refers to Christ freely rendering himself powerless.

"The condition of a slave" is a reference to our unredeemed human life or bondage ending in death before our situation is changed by Christ.

"Became as men are." In Greek this means, become an identical copy.

"Became obedient unto death" – death meaning not simply the terminal point of Christ's obedience, but the inevitable consequence of being both fully human and obedient *in a world alienated from God.*

"Death of a cross" indicates Christ experiencing the extremity of human abandonment.

Note the build up to verse 11 – "the name" (*Kyrios*). The words "Every knee should bend" (cf Isa 45:23) transfers to Jesus the homage given to God alone (thus adhering to strict monotheism) and the granting to him of universal Lordship (cf 1 Cor 3:21-23; Rom 14:9).

The ultimate goal of the hymn is to the glory of God.

Practical suggestions

1. Discover ways in which you can be of service to others, e.g. volunteer to work in your spare time in a charity shop or soup kitchen or some organisation for the homeless.

2. Locate and visit someone who is handicapped or housebound.

3. If it's not possible to do something suggested above, do include the sick, the lonely, the bereaved and those who have no faith in your prayers.

NOTE

1. Donald Nicholl. *The Beatitude of Truth: Reflections of a Life-time*, Ed. Adrian Hastings, DLT, 1997, pp160-161.

Chapter 3

The True Image of God

"He alone is God who can never be sought in vain; not even when he cannot be found."
(Bernard of Clairvaux)

The first problem we encounter when we wish to find and draw close to God on our own particular road through life, as well relate consciously with him on our journey, is the fact that he contradicts all our expectations as to what he is like. God the Father is certainly not – to put it crudely – an irascible old man with a long white beard, sitting on a cloud in judgement on us and wanting us to feel guilty. Neither does his Son, Jesus, fit easily into how we may visualise him. None of the images we also may have of him are adequate. He is neither just the possibly gentle Jesus, meek and mild of our childhood, nor solely the angry Jesus expelling the tradesmen and money changers from the temple, as so many of us choose to imagine him. Furthermore, once we discover that our ideas about God are inadequate, (they usually tell us more about ourselves than about God), we then learn that how he wishes us to behave is also not the usual way we do things in this world.

Whereas for example we may be desperately and understandably keen in our domestic lives to provide our families with what we call as high a standard of living as possible, this is not among God's priorities for us. We may wish to provide our children with the best and often most expensive education possible, endow our loved ones with as many of this world's glitzy goods as possible, ranging from the houses we live in, the cars we drive, to the number of holidays abroad that we take each year, these things simply do not interest God – except in so far as they affect how we either love or don't love him and other people.

What interests God is how we respond to his commandment first found in Deuteronomy 6:5 and echoed in Luke 10:27-28.

> "You must love the Lord your God with all your heart, with all your soul, with all your strength, and with all your mind, and your neighbour as yourself."

Additionally, whereas we may be ambitious and competitive in matters to do with our work, hoping to obtain promotion, an increase in power, prestige and pay, as well as sufficient money for when we retire, not to mention how we may fuss about the state of our health, worry as to how to pay off the mortgage, higher purchase payments, credit cards, and so on, Jesus, God's Son, made it clear where our priorities should be and strongly advised us against worrying about such matters.

He first speaks about the danger of avarice, telling his disciples that "a man's life is not made secure by what he owns, even when he has more than he needs." (Lk 12:13) Then, after telling them the parable of the rich man who had such a good harvest that he intended to tear down his barns and build bigger ones in which to store his grain, but then died before he could do so (Lk 12:16-21), Jesus went on to teach them to place their trust instead in providence.

"That is why I am telling you," he said, "not to worry about your life and what you are to eat, nor about your body and how you are to clothe it. For life means more than food, and the body more than clothing." (Lk 12:22-23)

It is actually in Jesus' birth in the stable at Bethlehem that we are given a clue as to the true nature of the God Christians worship. This tells us what God is like and how he acts, which is utterly contrary to human expectations and behaviour.

He is also a God of paradox. We would not expect God to become incarnate as a frail baby and become subject to all human limitations except that he did not sin. What could be more vulnerable or frail than a baby? We are much more likely to imagine God descending on earth amid a massive display of power and authority. However that is not his style.

As the source of all things, God both transcends all earthly assessments and experience and is incomparable in his immanence or ability, to be within us. As the prophet Isaiah recognised, God's thoughts are not our thoughts, his ways are not our ways (Isa 55:8). And as St Paul was to echo:

"How rich are the depths of God – how deep his wisdom and knowledge – and how impossible to penetrate his motives or understand his methods!

Who could ever know the mind of the Lord? Who could ever be his counsellor? Who could ever give him anything or lend him anything? All that exists comes from him; all is by him and for him." (Rom 11:33-36)

Even when Jesus made it clear to the apostle Philip that to have seen him was to have seen God, the Father, (Jn 14:9), it was only after his resurrection that Jesus' followers fully understood that he always had been the Word of God, true image of God. It was only later that Matthew and Luke incorporated into their gospels the Christmas stories, now with obvious emphasis on his poverty and weakness.

Both the birth at Bethlehem and death on the cross disclose the same secret about God. As St Paul told the people of Corinth, "God's foolishness is wiser than human wisdom, and God's weakness is stronger than human strength." (1 Cor 1:25)

"The great news of the Gospel," writes a modern writer, Henri Nouwen, "is precisely that God became small and vulnerable, and hence bore fruit among us… Jesus brought us new life in ultimate vulnerability. He came to us as a small child, dependent on the care and protection of others. He lived for us as a poor preacher, without any political, economic, or military power. He died for us nailed on a cross as a useless criminal. It is in this extreme vulnerability that our salvation was won."[1]

Indeed Christ's absolute humanity is the key to our understanding of what he did for us, how he rescued us, and how we were thereby redeemed. As is stated in the Second Vatican Council document, *Gaudium et Spes*, "Jesus worked with human hands, thought with a human mind, acted by human choice and loved with a human heart. He has truly been made one of us… The divinity of Christ is ever inseparable from his humanity."

Indeed, it is unlikely that reason, logic or the

imagination would ever have discovered this truth, for as Nouwen says in another context,

> "God cannot be understood; he cannot be grasped by the human mind. The truth escapes our human capacities… We can neither explain God nor his presence in history. As soon as we identify God with any specific event or situation, we play God and distort the truth. We only can be faithful in our affirmation that God has not deserted us but calls us in the middle of all the unexplainable absurdities of life."[2]

So because it is beyond the usual expectations of how God would act, what was God's motive at the incarnation? He did it entirely out of love, so much so that he also gave us consciousness and freedom. Even so, given the immense size of the universe, how can we as human beings possibly consider that we are important?

The Universe

From outer space our earth appears as one of nine planets belonging to and revolving round the sun. The latter is a great ball of fire, so immense that a million earths could fit inside it, but there is nothing special about the sun. Every star in the sky is a sun and simply appears small to us because they are far away.

The sun is a medium sized star much like others, situated in the outer parts of the Milky Way galaxy. This is a great flattened swirling disc composed of one hundred billion stars or twenty stars for every man, woman and child on earth. These stars also have planets circling them in the same way as our sun. Planetary systems are common and there's nothing special about our galaxy. There are others, estimated to number one hundred billion, that is twenty galaxies for every human being on earth.

Moreover, if we were to add together all the stars of all the galaxies, the total number in the universe would be, as one observer has said, "approximately the same as the number of grains of sand in a sandcastle five miles high by five miles wide by five miles long."

The galaxies occur in clusters of galaxies and are situated at great distances from us. Some are so far it takes almost twelve billion years for their light to reach us. In other words, the universe is huge and for all the influence we have on the motion of the stars and planets we might as well not exist. So, given the size of the universe, how can we as human beings think we are important?

It would seem that the sun is more essential than we are. We circle it, it does not circle us. If suddenly its fires were extinguished all life on earth would die. And yet we actually are important because we are conscious, we are aware of things, we have thoughts and feelings, whereas the sun doesn't know its importance, it doesn't know anything. It is not conscious.

Blaise Pascal once said "Man is the feeble reed in existence, but he is a thinking reed." We know we exist. Not a single one of the stars in the universe is aware that it exists. Size has nothing to do with it! And that's why God loves us. "We are God's work of art…" (Eph 2:10).

It is small wonder then that the Psalmist could cry out:

"When I see the heavens, the work of your
    hands,
the moon and the stars which you arranged,
what is man that you should keep him in
    mind,
mortal man that you care for him?
Yet you have made him little less than a god;
with glory and honour you crowned him,
gave him power over the works of your hand,
put all things under his feet."   (Psalm 8)

In our world, a world of famines, tsunamis, diseases, wars and violence, the only kind of God who makes sense is also the one never on the side of the powerful, and the one who identifies with the poor and the destitute. As Jesus made clear, when we fail to feed the hungry, give refreshment to the thirsty, welcome the stranger, clothe the naked, and visit those in prison or who are sick, we are neglecting God. (Mt 25:31-46).

If we turn to the Crucifixion we discover that almost one third of Mark's Gospel is devoted to the last five days of Jesus' life. In Paul's writings one gets the impression that he was not interested in Jesus' life between his birth and death! In fact the Gospels were in a sense written backwards. The accounts of the passion and death of Jesus constitute the oldest parts.

But why did Jesus become incarnate in order to die? As the *First Epistle of John* says, "God loved us and sent his Son to be the expiation for our sins." But why did he do this? He did it because our God is a forgiving and pardoning God. This is his nature. As the Psalmist wrote,

"God is tender and compassionate,
Slow to anger, most loving;
His indignation does not last for ever,
his resentment exists for a short time only;
he never treats us, never punishes us,
as our guilt and our sins deserve." (Psalm 103)

Incidentally this is not the same as being tolerant and is the opposite of over-looking wrong. Christians believe there is a moral order in our world, but God is the one who forgives and who, out of compassion and understanding of the wrong doer, accepts the wound and turns the evil into new life. Hence sacrifice is at the heart of God.

Christ also died for our regeneration or spiritual rebirth and in the process of baptism we become the adopted brothers and sisters of Christ. But to what extent is there sacrifice in our lives? To what degree do we die to self? Without sacrifice in our lives can we ever hope to draw close to God? In answering these questions it is the saints who show us the way.

Saints

We all know what it is like to look up to someone, to admire, respect and to wish to emulate such a person. When we are young they tend to be film stars, footballers or cricketers, pop stars, rock stars, soap actors or models. What today we call celebrities. As we get older and our perceptions change, we probably admire writers, painters and composers, experts in different fields of study, and, in the days when there seemed to be more of them about, statesmen, as distinct from politicians.

In the distant past, before the age of mass literacy

and communications, before television and radio, people were taught to have regard for saints. A third century theologian, called Irenaeus, once said that "the glory of God is a human being fully alive". That is what a saint is – someone fully alive in the fullest sense of the word and living now in the actual presence of God.

Saints vary enormously. Some have been missionaries, such as St Paul, some simple peasants, like Bernadette, and others have been Kings and Queens, such as St Margaret of Scotland. Some saints, such as St Christopher, are in fact legendary whilst others, such as St Thomas Becket, are important historical figures.

Many Christians pray to saints and seek their help as people who have preceded them to heaven, friends with whom they can communicate and from whom receive help, just as they do from earthly friends. They honour saints, treasure their earthly remains and possessions (rather like keepsakes or relics), and name their children and churches after them.

Christians are not alone in their veneration of saintly figures. Buddhists venerate their holy men and lamas. Hindus revere their gurus. Muslims have their close friends of God and Sufi masters. Jews have popular devotion to Abraham and Moses and their *T-saddi-kim* or "just men".

Saints are also traditionally patrons of various activities or things. For example St Anthony is prayed to when people lose things, St Francis of Assisi is the patron saint of animals, St Luke of artists and St Cecilia of musicians. Saints also have their own emblems or symbols, often associated with the manner in which they died and are depicted in their portraits.

St Catherine of Alexandria is usually shown with a spiked wheel. Philip Howard (Earl of Arundel) is traditionally painted as an Elizabethan gentleman, accompanied by the dog he had with him in prison, and St Isidore (patron of Madrid) as a farmer. St Denis (patron of Paris) is often shown as having his head cut off, St Thomas the Apostle with his finger in the side of Jesus, St Stephen with stones and St Sebastian with arrows.

To be declared a saint involves a long, arduous and rigorous examination of his or her words and deeds, character and intentions. And all of the way claims made on her or his behalf are scrutinised. It is not an easy process. Some candidates for sainthood never make it. Those who do make it are amazing. The poet W.H. Auden once said:

> "I have met in my life two persons, one a man, the other a woman, who convinced me that they were persons of sanctity. Utterly different in character, upbringing and interests as they were, their effect on me was the same. In their presence I felt myself to be ten times as nice, ten times as intelligent, ten times as good-looking as I really was."

That is the effect saints have on us. Whether they are on earth or in heaven they transform other people. To think, as some people do, that Christians worship saints is ridiculous! Saints are not the opposite of sinners, they are what Christians call saved sinners. We honour, respect and even love them, but as close friends. Their value for us today lies in their example, patronage, inspiration and ability to intercede for us. We strive to be like them. They are among the friends we hope to join one day in heaven. But worship is for God alone.

Every single human being is valuable, whether bright or stupid, beautiful or ugly, rich or poor, talented or otherwise. And the reason for this is because we're all made in the image of God. But equally we are all sinners, in other words we think, say and do things which are wrong and we sometimes neglect to do things which are right. Saints are those who realise that, because they're sinners, they need Jesus. And so they do something about it. Furthermore they don't do things by halves. But they remain utterly human. For example St Jerome was renowned for being cantankerous, St John the Baptist was a firebrand, St Augustine was often moody and St Teresa of Avila often impatient.

Saints are not the meek and mild people we might imagine from their pictures in stained glass or how they appear in statue form. Some of them were ferocious, some were great wits, some were dreamers and passionate poets, some former soldiers. What they have in common is their yearning for intimacy with God, their adherence to the faith, their perseverance in prayer and their love for their fellow human beings. This last quality is the most important. It's not possible to be a saint, let alone draw close to the God Christians worship, if we don't care for our fellow human beings.

St Francis of Assisi once asked: "Imagine you're standing before God in heaven and a tramp knocks at the door asking for a cup of water – What should you do?" The answer he gave was that, "you should turn away from God to help the tramp, because turning away from God to help the tramp is the real heaven. And if you were to ignore the tramp, you're actually turning away from God's face because a saint sees Jesus in the tramp."

There is a section in Thomas Merton's auto-biography, *The Seven Storey Mountain* where he remarks that the only worthwhile pursuit in life is to be a saint. This idea was originally put to him by his friend Robert Lax, who then advised Merton that, if he wanted to be a saint, then God would help him to become one. This is true for all of us and why Thérèse of Lisieux embarked on what she called her Little Way.

"You know I have always longed to be a saint," she once wrote, "but in comparing myself with the saints, I have always felt that I am so far removed from them as a grain of sand trampled under foot by a passer-by from the mountain whose summit is lost in the clouds." Then she continues, "Instead of feeling dis-couraged by such reflections, I came to the conclusion that God would not inspire a wish which could not be realised, and that in spite of my littleness I might aim at being a saint. It is impossible for me to become great, so I must bear with myself and my many imperfections, but I will seek out a means of reaching Heaven by a little way – very short, very straight and actually new."[3]

In a similar way this idea had been articulated by the nineteenth-century John Henry Cardinal Newman when he remarked,

"It is the saying of holy men, that if we wish to be perfect, we have nothing more to do than to perform the ordinary duties of the day well. A short road to perfection – short not because easy, but pertinent and intelligible... We must bear in mind what is meant by perfection. It does not mean any extraordinary service, anything out of the way, or especially heroic... He, then, is perfect who does the work of the day perfectly, and we need not go beyond this to seek for perfection. You need not go out of the round of the day."[4]

However, in order to find God in our usually busy everyday lives, we first need to understand like the saints that there is a certain disposition, attitude of mind and outlook that we must strive to cultivate. Unless we do this, like the disciples on the road to Emmaus, we too shall surely fail to recognise Jesus in the direction we happen to be going. In the following chapters, therefore, the qualities we need for our journey will be explored in some detail.

Questions to consider

1. What characteristics do we most associate with the person of Jesus?
2. Does our image of God coincide with that of Jesus in the Gospels?
3. How should we behave in order to become a saint?

Suggested Scriptural reading

St John's Gospel, chapter 14, verses 5-14. Jesus, the Way to the Father.

Practical ideas

1. Read the life of a saint that you admire and consider the value that his or her life might have on you personally. Go on to consider the value of praying to such a saint.

2. Consider visiting someone who is sick or offer to assist someone clearly in need of help.

NOTES

1. Henri Nouwen, *Jesus a Gospel,* Orbis Books, 2001, p.5.
2. Ibid., *The Genesee Diary,* Image Books, 1981, p.137.
3. Michael Hollings, *Thérèse of Lisieux,* Collins, 1981, p.38.
4. From *Meditations and Devotions,* 1893.

Chapter 4

The *Anawim* or Poor of God

"The love of worldly possessions is a sort of birdlime, which entangles the soul and prevents it flying to God."   (Augustine of Hippo)

Sixty years ago a Scottish couple, living in Glasgow, had no children of their own and decided to approach an Order of Nuns, who looked after abandoned children, in order to adopt a baby. The couple were as poor as church mice but devout Christians and wonderfully generous people. At the end of World War II the husband, a former soldier, was left with only one leg and one lung. His wife had extremely poor health and was constantly in and out of hospital. She had also had numerous miscarriages, so the couple assumed they would never be able to have children of their own. However a year after they had adopted a baby boy, the wife gave birth to a son. The family now numbered four.

All four lived, washed, cooked, ate their meals and slept in one room. They shared a lavatory on a landing with neighbours. The room however was not only spotlessly clean, but was a haven of happiness and laughter and the family were assiduous in their religious practices, attending Mass on Sundays and together saying their daily prayers. Then the woman's sister, who was a widow, died leaving two children, a girl and a boy. The couple took in the boy, so now there were five people living in that one room. This continued until the boys were in their late teens, when the family was finally allotted a council house. Each of the boys in turn left school at sixteen and sought work in order to help provide food for the family table and to assist with the rent. In his free time the adopted son began assisting the nuns in their work among children in care, as a way of paying back to society something of what he had received from his adoptive parents. Then, against all odds, he eventually became a qualified social worker.

It is highly doubtful if he, his brother, and cousin would even have survived in the beginning and early years without the care lavished on them, all living in one room, by the couple who brought them up and loved them unconditionally in a truly Christian context. The truth is that couple had so little of this world's goods that they had become totally reliant on God and realised it. Their commitment to Christ, born out of humble recognition of their need of him, was astonishing and accounted for their utter charity to not only their family but virtually all others too. They were of the *anawim*.

The *Anawim* or Poor of God

In the Old Testament the *anawim* or poor of God are those who, having been stripped of everything and sometimes sent into exile, came to place their hope and trust solely in God. They learnt the secret of power in weakness and glory through suffering (weakness in the sense of becoming pliant to God's ways and suffering in the sense of dying to self). And they are depicted in the Psalms as beggars before God, the opposite of the proud and self sufficient, to whom God is particularly close (Ps 21, 34, and 68).

It was of the *anawim* that Jeremiah was speaking when he declared in whom God would put his law and write it upon their hearts; that Isaiah declared to be the people to whom the Servant of the Lord, the Messiah, would come to preach the Good News; that Ezekiel had in mind, albeit unconsciously, when he prophesied concerning those to whom God would give a new heart and a new spirit (Jer 31:33; Isa 61:1; Ezek 36:26).

One of the most typical of the poor of God in the New Testament is the Virgin Mary. Generally speaking there can be few stronger bonds than those that exist between a child and his or her mother. When one is a child it is to one's mother that one usually instinctively turns for food, protection and love. When one is either misunderstood or let down, one can nevertheless usually depend on one's mother for comfort. Whatever one's situation one can for the most part rely on one's mother to stand by one to provide shelter, if not always understanding. Even to imagine one's mother being hurt, endangered, insulted, neglected or badly treated is often enough to make one spring into defensive action. That which binds a person to his or her mother is frequently so strong that it defies adequate description. So how can one begin to comprehend how strong must have been the relationship between Jesus and his mother?

It is absolutely true that Jesus is "the key, the focal point, and the goal of all human history" (*Gaudium et Spes*, 10). Nevertheless, if we wonder how we may love God with all our heart, soul, mind and strength, all we have to do is to take a hard look at how Jesus' mother behaved at the Annunciation, the birth of Jesus, and as she uttered her Magnificat, as well as listen to what she said at the wedding feast in Cana ("Do whatever he [Jesus] tells you.") and observe how she suffered at the foot of the cross of her son. These are all occasions which identify Mary as being one of the *anawim*, quite apart from being events in her life which have tested the talents of artists, poets and musicians down the centuries. That is why the distinguished theologian, Hans Von Balthasar, can say "The veneration of Mary is the surest and shortest way to get close to Christ in a concrete way." Indeed Mary's whole life and stance personifies the *anawim*. It is also the *anawim* that Jesus had in mind when speaking of what we call the Beatitudes.

The Beatitudes

These occur twice in the New Testament, in the Gospels of Luke and Matthew and are frequently a puzzle to people. The Beatitudes reflect God's attitude towards those who behave as God wishes them to behave. They are also words of encouragement. They are called Beatitudes from the word *makarios* (Greek) meaning blessed.

It is wrong incidentally to translate the word *makarios* as happy. The etymological root of *happy* is *hap* and means by *chance*. Blessedness is not a matter of chance! The Blessed are those who will be rewarded by God at the end of time and the Beatitudes reflect the three virtues of Christian life, mercy, purity and peacemaking. When reading the Beatitudes, we should remember that the kingdom of God is already here, not just somewhere in the future. It is wherever people are doing the will of God.

3. "Blessed are the poor in spirit, for theirs is the kingdom of heaven."

   This raises the question why are the poor blessed? It is because they recognise their need of God. They are the *anawim*. They don't depend solely on their own efforts. They're the ones who will enter the Kingdom of God.

4. "Blessed are those who mourn, for they shall be comforted." Mourn in Matthew's gospel means not simply for the dead but for the human condition. In other words, those who are sad on account of the state of the world. It is they who will be comforted.

5. "Blessed are the meek, for they shall inherit the earth."

6. "Blessed are those who are hunger and thirst for righteousness, for they shall be satisfied."

7. "Blessed are the merciful, for they shall obtain mercy."

8. "Blessed are the pure in heart, for they shall see God."

9. "Blessed are the peacemakers, for they shall be called sons of God."

10. "Blessed are those who are persecuted for righteousness' sake, (for a life pervaded by God), for theirs is the kingdom of heaven."

11. "Blessed are you when they revile you and persecute you and utter all kinds of evil against you falsely on my account."

12. "Rejoice and be glad, for your reward is great in heaven, for so they persecuted the prophets who were before you."

(Matthew 5:3-12)

By contrast those who now are rich, having their fill, enjoying themselves now, that is placing their trust in material possessions and this world's goods instead of God, will experience the opposite when Christ returns in judgment. As will those thought highly of by those who judge through worldly eyes.

In a very real sense the Beatitudes sum up Jesus' teaching and provoke such questions as to whether or not we are following this teaching in our daily lives and whether we place our trust in God or ourselves? If not, is that a reason which contributes to our not recognising Christ as often as we should in our daily lives as we journey through life?

Jesus as one of the Poor of God

When thinking of Jesus as the one who fulfilled Isaiah's prophecy of a suffering servant, it is important to see him as one who allied himself with the *anawim*. Thomas Merton tells us this when he says:

"Into this world, this demented inn, in which there is absolutely no room for Him at all, Christ has come uninvited. But because He cannot be at home in it, because He is out of place in it, His place is with those for whom there is no room. His place is with those who do not belong, who are rejected by power because they are regarded as weak, those who are discredited, who are denied the status of persons, (those unjustly accused and con-demned). With those for whom there is no room, Christ is present in the world. He is mysteriously present in those for whom there seems nothing but the world at its worst… It is in these that He hides himself, for whom there is no room." *(Raids on the Unspeakable)*

So it was that St Paul could rejoice and write to the people of Corinth:

> "So I shall be happy to make my weaknesses my special boast so that the power of Christ may stay over me, and that is why I am quite content with my weaknesses, and with insults, hardship, persecutions and with the agonies I go through for Christ's sake. For it is when I am weak that I am strong." (2 Cor12:9-10)

Again the question arises, are we like this or are we by nature comfort seeking creatures? Perhaps by inclination we don't like facing problems or difficulties, don't like dying to ourselves, being unselfish and emptied of self to give room to God. Perhaps we wrap ourselves up in the flimsy garments of our own right-eousness and then too often complain of the cold!

We hear a great deal today about the state of the Church in the West, such things as declining numbers of people attending church, the shortage of vocations to the priesthood and religious life, the scandal of paedophilia, the decline in Europe at least of the influence of the Christian faith on events, and the advance of secularism in the West. In view of these things one is sometimes compelled to ask whether it is God's will that the institutional Church should shrink and become instead a community of *anawim,* a people totally dependent on Him?

Certainly Benedict XVI in *Salt of the Earth,* written before he became Pope, remarked that the Church of the future would assume different forms. He said,

"She will be less identified with the great societies, more a minority Church; she will live in small, vital circles of really convinced believers who live their faith. But precisely in this way she will, biblically speaking, become the salt of the earth again."

Then, when examining Western society, we read a great deal about consumerism, the cult of celebrity, the culture of death (abortion and euthanasia), the technological and communications revolution (computers, mobile phones, iPods, e-mailing, digital television and cameras). When looking at the world as a whole we hear so much about globalisation, climate change, violence, terrorism and war, the huge waves of immigration taking place, the industrial explosion in India and China, and poverty in Africa. All this sometimes seems enough to make one despair, but the truth is we can do nothing of worth concerning any of these things unless we first become as the *anawim*. Or as Thomas Merton once wrote:

"Just as the Word emptied Himself of His divine and transcendent nobility in order to 'descend' to the human level, so we must empty ourselves of what is human in the ignoble sense of the word , which really means what is less than human."

Until we do that in our daily lives as individuals and as a community, our efforts to recognise Christ on our own Road to Emmaus will fail.

Points for reflection

1. To what extent do we appreciate our need of God? In other words, how like are we to the *anawim*?

2. To what extent are we influenced by materialism?

Suggested Scriptural reading

St Mark's Gospel, chapter 12, verses 41-44. The Widow's Offering.

Practical ideas

1. The next occasion we go shopping, let's ask ourselves whether we actually need those things we are purchasing and let's consider by contrast the situation of so many in the developing world.

2. Consider what we do in our daily lives which enable us to practise self-denial.

Chapter 5

The Presence of Christ

"Test yourselves to see if you are living the life of faith: practise discernment. Are you not yourselves aware that Christ Jesus is in you?" (2 Cor 13:5)

Strange though it may sound, unless we cultivate intimacy in our relationship with God, we shall never draw close to him, let alone recognise him in all the events of our every day lives on our journey. So how may we achieve this?

In *The Times* newspaper of 7 April 2007 it was reported that the Archbishop of Birmingham, Vincent Nichols, (now Archbishop of Westminster), "sells God". The reporter said there was "no other way of putting it." "He sells God by making him hot."

At his Chrism Mass in Holy Week that year we are told that the archbishop said to the congregation, "The Almighty awaits our 'Yes' just as much as a young bridegroom awaits the yes of his bride… He longs to draw us to Himself." He went on to tell the congregation that they should "be filled" by God, "with the recklessness of lovers." Whether or not he realised it, the archbishop was here echoing the words of St John Climacus, who wrote, "Blessed is the person whose desire for God has become like the lover's passion for the beloved."[1]

The Times described the archbishop's words as steamy stuff. The archbishop insists, it went on, that faith should be physically passionate. "Why not?" asks the archbishop in a subsequent interview. "The crucifix is pretty physical, a physical expression of love. In that sense religion is not so abstract. It's maybe not physical in a genital way but sex is more than intercourse, it's the whole thing that says we two belong to each other."

But how is this relevant to us as we endeavour to draw close to Christ on our journey, like that of the two disciples on their way to Emmaus?

One of the major differences between human animals and other animals is their use of language. Whereas other animals, from whales to ants and bees, have systems of communication, only humans employ intelligent reasoned speech and indeed laughter, or try to provoke us into thinking as the archbishop does.

As mentioned earlier, only we humans have self awareness and can, as it were, stand outside ourselves, see ourselves for what we are and have consciences. Whereas you and I know we are human, cows, rabbits, foxes, deer and birds do not know they are such. Their knowledge is infinitely less and is restricted to being aware among other things, for example, of when danger is close, in the form of a larger predator than themselves.

Given this fact that being human is something unique, our ability to speak and use language (both spoken and written) is something wonderful. What we say and write can have immense significance. One has only to think how marvellous human communication is in these days of modern technological advances.

We can learn what is happening all around the world by listening to the news on television or radio in a matter of minutes, if not seconds, as was clear on

9/11 and the terrorist attack on the twin towers. On an individual level, think what a difference the three words "I love you" (when uttered seriously and taken as such) can make to a relationship between two people. Indeed language is a truly amazing facility.

In St Paul's Letter to the Galatians (1:15-16) there is an arresting phrase. Paul says that God was pleased "to reveal his Son *in me*." This more than suggests a personal intimacy with Christ. It is reflected elsewhere in Paul's letters when he uses the expression "in Christ" and "in Christ Jesus". It indicates Paul's awareness of Christ's abiding presence.

In the same Letter to the Galatians (2:20) Paul also describes his tremendous sense of a new life imparted to him by his experience on the road to Damascus. "It is no longer I that live Christ lives in me!" he declares. In Romans 6:23 he writes of the enormous gift God has conferred on him – "the charism of God is eternal life in Christ Jesus our Lord." He ascribes the beginning and continuance of his Christian life to the initiative of the Father and the activity of the risen Lord. He goes on to consider that the presence within him of the living Christ is the powerful, dynamic presence of the Father in his Christian life. To live "in Christ Jesus" is in fact "living for God" (Rom 6:11).

It is this vital and intense awareness of his relationship with Christ, the Christ he had met on the road to Damascus, that keeps Paul continuously aware of the presence of God in his life and all his apostolic work. In his Second Letter to the Corinthians (2:17) Paul says: It is as coming from God that we, *in Christ*, proclaim (the word) in the presence of God." (Paul is totally aware of how the presence of God in the Old Testament Psalms was described as being found in the sanctuary and religious rites of the temple [Ps 48, 24, 29, and 114].) But this is more intimate and what are the practical implications of all this for us?

In his First Letter to the Thessalonians (5:19-22) Paul writes: "Do not quench the Spirit; do not belittle prophetic utterances, test everything about them; hold on to what is good, shun every appearance of evil (in them)."

He warns the Romans (8:9-10) "If a man has not Christ's spirit, he does not belong to his party. But if Christ *is within you*, your body is dead so far as sin is concerned and your spirit is alive with regard to uprightness."

In writing to the Colossians (1:26-27) Paul speaks of this presence of Christ as the great Christian mystery, "the Mystery concealed for ages and generations, but now manifested to his saints, to whom God has determined to disclose the riches of the glory of this mystery among the pagans, I mean, *Christ in you*, the hope of glory."

Finally, on the matter of being *in Christ,* it is clear that, from the time of his encounter with Christ on the road to Damascus, Paul embarked on a voyage of discovery that carried him all through his life and beyond, to an ever deepening understanding of what it meant to know and be with Christ. By comparison with which all else was – as he said – so much rubbish.

The fact is being *in Christ* was the basis of Paul's prayer life and hopefully it is ours. Paul was fully aware that, without recourse to prayer, the first and second greatest commandments, to love God and to love one's neighbour, could not be kept, hence his frequent instruction to the early Christians that they should pray.

Just as much it is safe to say that without prayer, especially when we perform acts greatly appreciated in the eyes of others, we may delude ourselves into believing that we ourselves are the complete authors of our achievements. We shall then fail to understand that we are simply instruments in God's hands. Prayer not only brings us close to God but enables us to recognise that we are his creatures.

Prayer

"Rejoice always", Paul told the Thessalonians (1 Thess 5:16-18) pray constantly, give thanks in all circumstances."

To the Romans (12:12) he wrote, "Do not give up if trials come; and keep on praying."

And to the Ephesians (6:18) he instructed that they should "Pray all the time, asking for what they need praying in the Spirit on every possible occasion."

All of which is totally out of the question if viewed *solely* as an exercise requiring a great many words, instead of our being involved in a relationship of love with God (hence my earlier quotation from the archbishop). And therefore, as in all matters of genuine love, won't there be ebbs and flows? Surely this is part of the human condition?

Since we are creatures with instincts and emotions, as well as minds and wills, surely we should expect periods of dryness, monotony and fatigue, as well as times of consolation in our prayer lives? Simply being aware of God at all times that we are awake, however, is a quite different matter. That should be our goal.

An aid to continuous prayer is what is known as the Jesus Prayer – "Lord, Jesus Christ, Son of God, have mercy on me a sinner." This is at the heart of a book that comes out of Eastern Orthodoxy, called *The Way of the Pilgrim,* which encourages the reader to use this prayer at all times. For us it is exceedingly useful when we are walking for example from one place to another, standing in a queue for a bus or to be served, waiting for an appointment or simply pausing between activities. If we carefully examine the meaning of each word of the prayer as we slowly recite it, not only are we keeping God consciously in our minds but enriching them.

This is so even though, as we saw in a previous chapter, no two people will ever pray in exactly the same way. But why should they? There is perhaps only one rule concerning prayer which applies to us all; we should pray as we are, where we are, and never give up. And in answer to any question concerning the nature of the God that we pray to, we simply need to consider how Jesus himself prayed.

Jesus at prayer

From the Gospels we know that, as a devout and practising Jew, Jesus attended worship in his local synagogue and at the Temple in Jerusalem and would have been steeped in the writings of the Old Testament prophets. He therefore understood the value of community prayer. Even so, Jesus demonstrated in his own life how seriously he regarded personal prayer, especially in relation to God his Father.

Frequently we read how, "Very early next morning

he [Jesus] got up and went to a lonely spot and remained there in prayer" (Mk 1:35). Similarly, following the first miracle of the loaves and fishes and after sending the crowds away, he went up into the hills to pray (Mt 14:13ff); a practice he was to repeat often. So in our regular withdrawal from our activities in order to pray and reflect, we are simply following his example.

Towards the end of his life Jesus showed how profoundly indeed he valued prayer when, in the Garden of Gethsemane, he wrestled with an inner conflict (Mt 26: 36-46). Moreover, even in his agony Jesus was bent solely on seeking the will of his Father. "Father," he said, "if you are willing, take this cup away from me. Nevertheless, let your will be done, not mine" (Lk 22:42).

In his teaching on prayer Jesus was insistent on the need for humility. This is particularly shown in the story in which he contrasts the hypocrisy of the Pharisee with the humility of the tax collector. (Lk 18:9-14) He taught that we should pray to the Father with complete confidence (Mt 7:7-11); that we should pray with persistence (Lk 11:5-58 and 18:1-8); and with assurance that our prayers will be answered (Jn 15:7, 17). Concerning the end of the world, Jesus advised his disciples to "Stay awake, praying at all times for the strength to survive all that is going to happen" (Lk 21:36).

Above all, on the occasion when his disciples had seen Jesus at prayer and asked him to teach them to pray, he gave them the Our Father. For many people this is the first prayer they remember being taught and saying. Alongside the Hail Mary or Jesus Prayer, it is possibly the Christian prayer most often recited throughout the world. Because it is so familiar however we perhaps sometimes say it without thinking. It may be helpful therefore if we examine it in detail and seek each part of the prayer's relevance to our own individual lives.

Our Father

As Jesus was a Jew it is not surprising that the form of the Lord's Prayer, found in the Gospels of Matthew and Luke, often parallels that found in Jewish prayers of his time. But have we noticed the teaching with which Jesus surrounds the Our Father?

In Matthew – written for a specifically Jewish audience – Jesus follows the Jewish tradition of speaking of almsgiving, prayer and fasting, with emphasis on all three being pursued in secret (Mt 6:1-18). In Luke – written with a Gentile audience in mind – the Our Father is immediately followed by an emphasis on persistence in prayer and an assurance that prayer is effective (Lk 11: 5-13).

"Our Father"

For Jesus to use the word *Father* in a prayer was his most usual custom. The only occasion when he does otherwise is from the cross when he quotes Psalm 22 and cries out "My God, my God…" Whatever word Jesus used in Aramaic for Father, it is not disputed that he intended it to convey warmth and intimacy without being disrespectful.

When we begin the prayer we approach God as our Father, the source of life and goodness, who sent his only Son into our world for our sake because he loves us so much.

Incidentally, the Church has persisted in retaining the word "our" before "Father", something not found in Luke. This enables us to bear in mind that God is the father of all people, not simply ourselves. It is not an emphasis on masculinity but on God's creative powers.

"Who art in heaven"

God is spirit and not confined to a place in the earthly sense of the word. When we say that God is "in heaven" this tells us much more about who he is. He is wherever there is good including in our lives.

"Hallowed be thy name"

Among the Jews the name of a person was not used simply to enable them to address someone. For them it referred to their character and even nature. In reference to God therefore it was supremely important, so much so that they refused to call God by his name. Reverence for the name of God was made explicit in the Ten Commandments (Ex 20:7) and to hallow God's name is for us an attempt to approach him in a manner as worthy as possible in accordance with who he is.

"Thy Kingdom come (Thy will be done on earth as it is in heaven)"

This petition is typically Jewish in that it is closely linked to what goes before and after it. Since God is our Father and creator we desire that he should reign in our hearts and minds. (The phrase which follows in Matthew but which is omitted in Luke – "thy will be done on earth as it is in heaven" – is equally a logical follow on.)

Reference to the kingdom is obviously not a geographical expression, but more a reference to the rule of God or, better still, his reign over us and his world. The term kingdom in this sense occurs frequently in the Gospels and has strong roots in the Old Testament. Having earlier spoken of God's name and nature, it is natural now to speak of his authority and will and to ask ourselves the extent to which they govern our lives.

So far in our consideration of the Lord's Prayer phrase by phrase, we have been concerned for the Person of God and have not formally prayed for ourselves or petitioned God for our own needs. Now we continue to examine the prayer phrase by phrase, but this time with our own needs in mind. This order of things is precisely as things should be in our actual lives, placing God first and only then ourselves. This was the order of things taught by Jesus.

"Give us this day our daily bread"

Origen, a theologian of the early Church (185-254 AD), maintained that the word "daily" was unknown both in Greek literature and usage, but Greek was the language in which the Gospels were written. It is now thought that its original usage by Jesus in the Our Father, spoken in Aramaic, was intended by him to mean that we should want for nothing today and be free of worry about tomorrow. This would certainly tie in with the teaching of Jesus that we should not be excessively concerned about material things or worry about the future, but place our trust in God (Mt 6:25-34).

As we pray this section for our needs we might pause and reflect on how we regard material things and our responsibility for people in the developing world. Do we place too much emphasis on our own material needs and do we sufficiently assist others less well off? And do we also regard other things such as peace and good relationships within the family as much part of our daily bread as actual edible food?

"And forgive us our trespasses, as we forgive those who trespass against us and lead us not into temptation, but deliver us from evil."

The word sin is not one most people nowadays use in everyday speech. Mistakes, failings, hurtful actions and so on are our more usual ways of speaking. It is the same with assigning responsibility for our personal weaknesses. Instead of taking the blame ourselves, we nowadays frequently accredit sin not to individual responsibility but instead to background, upbringing or lack of education.

This was not how Jesus regarded the matter. For him sin was an offence against God and a misuse of our God-given gift of free will. (Sin as an obstacle in the path of our meeting Jesus will be the subject of a later chapter.) Indeed the seriousness with which Jesus regarded sin and how he spent much of his time and energy forgiving people their sins caused hostility among the religious leaders at the time. Jesus, the Son of God, was so concerned about our sinfulness that he was prepared to sacrifice his life on our behalf in order that we might be forgiven.

Jesus was equally adamant that the degree to which we forgive others the offences they commit against us is the degree to which God will forgive us (Mt 18:23-35). In many ways this section of the Lord's Prayer makes for very sober praying. We cannot avoid seeing its relevance to our daily lives.

Finally, to pray not to be led into temptation, or as some translations have it, put us not to the test, and then to go on to pray to be delivered from evil (or the evil one) are basically cries for help.

Temptation is part of the human condition, a result of having free will and to being constantly under pressure to do the opposite of good. It is what we do with our temptations that is important. Given the nature of society and culture today, either hostile or indifferent to faith, Gerald O'Collins tells us in his book, *The Lord's Prayer*, that "in particular, we should pray to be preserved from giving up faith in Christ." We therefore need God's assistance to stand firm, not to give in to temptation and to resist evil.

To meditate upon the relevance of the Lord's Prayer to our daily lives, and then to incorporate our thoughts and concerns into a slow and careful utterance of the prayer as it was taught by Jesus, has brought comfort and consolation to millions of people down the centuries. It will do the same for us, provided we persevere in saying it and do so with total sincerity.

Jesus was absolutely certain of the effectiveness of prayer as when he told his followers that if they asked it would be given them, if they searched they would find, and if they knocked the door would always be opened to them (Lk 11:9-10).

We should be reassured immensely by how Jesus described the father (meaning God) in the parable of the prodigal son. "While he was still a long way off, his father saw him (the prodigal son) and was moved to pity. He ran to the boy, clasped him in his arms and kissed him tenderly" (Lk 15:20). It is clear that, such was the love between the father and the prodigal that words were in a sense superfluous.

Our prayer lives can be hugely fortified, deepened and even transformed by a specific type of reading known to monks and nuns as *Lectio Divina*[2]. This is a type of reading, especially of the Scriptures, geared particularly to enabling us to develop our relationship with God. Ideally it assists us to discover things not only about God but also about ourselves. At the same time as we read of and ponder on events, ideas, situations and attitudes in the Bible, so we are able personally to identify with them in our own lives. Using the image of eating, the Carthusian monk, Guigo, applies it to the different stages of 'digesting' a text.

> "Reading, as it were, puts the food into the mouth; meditation chews it and breaks it up; prayer extracts its flavour; contemplation is the sweetness itself which gladdens and refreshes."

The importance of silence

In the presence of people we love, surely at different times we experience being distracted, irritated, and moody, sometimes we are talkative, but then there are also times when we enjoy periods of utter silence; a silence nevertheless which is not an emptiness but an occasion of intimate understanding. Jesus himself said, "In your prayers do not babble as the pagans do, for they think that by using many words they will make themselves heard" (Mt 6:7).

Certainly in our prayer the value of silence cannot be over-estimated. This is an idea to which St Gregory the Great so often returned.

"For it is not our words that make the stronger impression on the ears of God, but our desires. Thus, if we seek eternal life with the mouth, but do not really desire it with the heart, when we cry out we are really silent. But, if we desire in the heart, even when our mouth is silent, in our silence we cry aloud…And the voice is heard in secret, when it cries out in silence with holy desires."[3]

St Anthony of Egypt, who valued silence, was of the view that, "The one who sits in solitude and quiet has escaped from three wars: hearing, speaking and seeing; yet against one thing shall he continually battle: that is in his own heart (his own demons)."

The writer Karl Adam once said, "Prayer is the meeting of the human personality with the divine, in a great silence where all else is hushed, for God is speaking." Silent union was equally advocated by the hermit martyr Charles de Foucauld who once remarked that "Prayer is that state in which the soul looks wordlessly on God, solely occupied with contemplating him."

What so many writers on prayer emphasise is that noise and restlessness are anathema to prayer. We seem however to live in an age when both predominate. In so many places, such as restaurants, background music has become the norm, whilst in the streets or on public transport, people are frequently either plugged into walkmans or chattering over mobile telephones. It's as if we are afraid of silence.

It is the same with movement. For how long can we sit completely still? Even after the briefest of time we feel the need either to move or to fidget. Pascal once said that, "All the miseries of mankind arise from man's inability to sit still in his own room."

On the other hand, neither noise nor movement are as powerful distractions to prayer as our thoughts. Not a moment goes by but our brains are active with our imaginings, our desires, our worries, our needs, our plans, our hopes and our fears.

Even away from the constant noise of city life, it is not always easy to achieve silence, stillness and inner quiet. Even there our imaginations are still at work. Long ago the Psalmist urged that we should be still in order that we may know God (Ps 46:10). So what are we to do?

In the Christian tradition it is those people called *hesychasts*, (from the Greek word *hesychia*, meaning quietness), who have specialised in the connection between prayer and silence. Such fourteenth-century writers as St Gregory of Sinai, St Nicephorus and St Gregory of Palamas especially taught the need to discipline the mind and body in order to assist the growth of spirituality in an individual. It was arguably the greatest heir of their teaching however, St Seraphim of Sarov (1759-1833), who made their ideas available to lay people.

After ordination to the priesthood and having immersed himself in the writings of the *hesychasts*, Seraphim spent ten years alone as a hermit in the woods near his monastery, after which ill health compelled him to return to life in community.

The core of Seraphim's teaching remains for us in what is known as *The Conversation of St Seraphim with Nicholas Motovilov*. Here he speaks of the need to so train the mind that it "swims" as it were in the law of God. He tells us that by not judging and by maintaining silence the peace of our souls will be preserved. He calls the mind of an attentive person a "sentry" and "sleepless guardian over the inner Jerusalem" and he teaches that, "Most of all must a man adorn himself with silence. As Ambrose of Milan says, by silence have I seen many saved, by many words, none."

Elsewhere Seraphim tells us that "Silence is the cross on which a man must crucify his ego" and how it "transfigures" a man into an angel. He teaches that the spiritual practice of silence preserves inner peace. Seraphim's teaching is as relevant today as ever. Incidentally, it is of more than passing concern that silence is highly valued for example in such Eastern religions as Hinduism and Buddhism. This is referred to in Donald Nicholl's classic, *Holiness*. In this, Nicholls tells of how he enquired of an Indian *muni* or holy man, who had not spoken for over a quarter of a century, what was the effect of living under a vow of silence. The *muni* gave his opinion, in writing on a chalk board, that he was soon made to realise how easily and frequently human beings speak for no good reason but simply as a means of indulging their egotism.

As a remedy for verbiage, which he describes as "the mark of a person who is full of himself", Nicholls recommends that we empty ourselves of our preoccupations and that we discriminate about what we allow to occupy our minds. He is emphatic that, "Emptiness, stillness, silence, each of these words is an attempt to pin-point the condition in which God is known." We are here reminded of an earlier chapter, where the value of *kenosis* or self-emptying was shown.

Finally, we might profit from studying the words of Bishop Theophan the Recluse on our approach to contemplative prayer.

> "In purely contemplative prayer, "he writes, "words and thought themselves disappear, not by our own wish, but of their own accord. Prayer of the mind changes into prayer of the heart…From now on in the usual course of spiritual life there is no other prayer. This prayer, taking deep root in the heart, may be without words or thought: it may consist only in standing before God, in an opening of the heart to Him in reverence and love."[4]

Without real prayer we most assuredly will neither recognise Christ in any meaningful way in our lives, nor be able to establish an intimate loving relationship with him as our Creator. We must persevere in prayer and so accompany Jesus on our particular Road to Emmaus in our daily lives.

Points for reflection

1. Slowly and carefully reflect upon the meaning of each part of the Lord's Prayer.

2. Examine your life and ask yourself whether or not there is sufficient silence in it and whether or not you are comfortable with silence.

Suggested Scriptural reading

Psalm 24, "To you, O Lord, I lift up my soul" and Psalm 50, "Have mercy on me, God, in your kindness."

Practical suggestions

1. Consider joining or forming a prayer group in your parish.
2. Spend part of each day quietly considering your priorities in life.

NOTES

1. John Climacus (c 570–c 649), *The Ladder of Divine Ascent,* in *Classics of Western Spirituality,* ed., Colm Luibheid and Norman Russell, Paulist Press, 1982.
2. For a fuller understanding of *Lectio Divina*, it is recommended that the reader should consult the many thoughtful articles on the subject by Fr Luke Dysinger OSB, located on the internet under his name.
3. Gregory the Great, *Moralia in Job*, editions available today – see the internet.
4. *The Art of Prayer, An Orthodox Anthology*, edited by Timothy Ware, Faber and Faber Ltd., 1966, p.72.

Chapter 6

Authentic Prayer
and the Role of Holy Spirit

"The angel answered (Mary) 'The Holy Spirit will come on you, and God's power will rest upon you. For this reason the holy child will be called the Son of God." (Lk 1:35)

How do we know whether or not our prayer is genuine and authentic? How can we tell whether or not we are fooling ourselves, or even deluding ourselves as we make our way on the road of life?

One sure sign is that we are at peace with God or as St Paul tells the Colossians: "The peace that Christ gives is to be the judge in your hearts…" This is not the same thing as saying we are necessarily and outwardly at ease with ourselves. Indeed we may be in the midst of turmoil in our daily life, but remain calm and at peace within.

The nature of the peace experienced when one has taken seriously the words, "Be still and know that I am God", or Jesus' thrice repeated words to his disciples after his resurrection, "Peace be with you", has been described in down to earth words by Abbot John Chapman in his *Spiritual Letters*.

"It is not a peace," says Chapman, "which is felt (emotionally, sensibly), but super-sensibly. If you try to translate it into language, you may find yourself saying something like this – 'What does it all matter? What does it matter whether

I enjoy Mass, or feel distracted or annoyed? What do my feelings matter? I came here for God, not myself. What do I matter? Only God matters. The whole world doesn't matter. Glory to God, that is the whole of everything.' And you look down at your soul, with a sort of amused pity, as a little wriggling worm, that won't keep still." [1]

A second sign that our prayer life is authentic is a willingness to allow God to do with us whatever he wills.

"You are the block," writes Abbot Chapman, "God is the sculptor; you cannot know what he is hitting you for, and you never will in this life."

This is the equivalent of what is sometimes termed abandonment to divine providence. 'Abandonment' in the Old Testament was strongly illustrated in the life of Abraham when he was prepared at God's instigation to leave his homeland, and in his willingness even to sacrifice his son, Isaac, at God's command (Gen 12:23). When it was made clear that God was actually only testing Abraham's obedience and Isaac was not required to be sacrificed, God rewarded Abraham for being prepared to trust God through thick and thin. "Because you have not refused me your son," said God, "your only son, I will shower blessings on you. I will make your descendants as many as the stars of heaven and the grains of sand on the seashore."

This reminds us of St Bernard's remark that it was not Christ's death that pleased the Father, so much as his willingness to die, or St Catherine of Siena's remark that it was not nails that held Christ to the cross but love. But to what extent do we abandon ourselves to the will of God? Isn't trust a required element in any meaningful relationship, including one with God?

The third indication as to whether or not we are genuinely praying is the experience of participating in an intimate and reciprocal relationship with a Person.

For different people this might be any one of the three Persons in the Trinity – the Person of God the Father, Jesus Christ or the Holy Spirit, and since God is both transcendent and not subject to our limitations, as well as being immanent or present in our depths, a fourth sign is an awareness of our own utter creatureliness; a realisation that persuades us to "surrender" to him.

It is then that we realise the truth of Jesus' words: "If anyone loves me he will keep my word and my Father will love him, and we shall come to him and make our home with him" (Jn 14:23). It is this that gives a Christian the driving force to endure calmly the trials and tribulations associated with being one of God's poor or one of the "*anawim*".

A fifth sign of the authenticity of our prayer lives is our intuitive understanding of St Paul's words that everyone moved by the Spirit is a son of God. Indeed the more we turn to the Holy Spirit the more important becomes prayer.

The Holy Spirit

Only in comparatively recent times have western Christians become more aware of the Holy Spirit as a living and vital Person in their lives. Even in the Eastern Orthodox Church, the doctrine of the Holy

Spirit is acknowledged to have the character of a secret, partially revealed, tradition.

Of the Three Persons of the Trinity the Holy Spirit seems to many of us the most vague and the most difficult to relate to from our experience of relationships. The dilemma for so many is how to relate with a Spirit as distinct from someone made of flesh and blood, someone we can see and touch?

To assist our understanding, Yves Congar, in his book *I believe in the Holy Spirit* once gave a list of those biblical archetypal symbols that reveal the nature of the Holy Spirit. Among them he listed wind, breath, water and fire, a cloud and a pillar of fire, the "finger" of God, and the seal and gift of the Father and Son to us. If we use the model provided by the twelfth-century Richard of St Victor, however, perhaps we get closer to discerning the Holy Spirit's value in our lives.

"When one gives love to another," says Richard, "and when he alone loves the other alone, there is love certainly but not shared love. When two love each other and give each other their most ardent affection, and when the affection of the first flows to the second and that of the second to the first, moving as it were in different directions, there is love on both sides certainly, but there is not shared love. Strictly speaking, there is shared love when two persons love a third in a harmony of affections and a community of love they have for the third... From this, then, it is evident that shared love would not have a place in the divinity if there were only two persons and not a third."[2]

Incidentally this explanation is echoed by C.S. Lewis in his *Four Loves*. The idea of shared love culminating in procreation is also one of the purposes of Christian marriage.

The great Russian saint, Seraphim of Sarov once defined the aim of the Christian life as "the acquisition of the Holy Spirit" and by studying how God gradually revealed the Spirit's existence in Scripture, so our prayer lives can become more meaningful.

In the Old Testament God's spirit is seen at creation as the source of life, hovering over the face of the waters (Gen 1:2) and quickening life in the inert body of the first man (Gen 2:7). The Spirit was with Bezalel and Oholiab when they constructed the Ark (Ex 36:1), with Joshua (Deut 34:9), and with such Judges as Gideon and Samson (Judg 6.34; 15:14). Prophets such as Ezekiel regarded possession of God's spirit as essential for his prophetic mission (Ezek 11:24-25). It was generally believed that the looked-for Messiah would possess the Spirit to the full (Isa 42:1) and the Messianic Age would witness an enormous outpouring of the Spirit (Joel 3:1-5).

In the New Testament, especially in the Gospels, there is progression in understanding of the Holy Spirit, whilst continuity with Old Testament ideas was maintained by reference to "overshadowing" by the Holy Spirit as in the context of Gabriel's message to Mary and by reference to a "cloud" as at the transfiguration and ascension of Christ. Both these expressions would have reminded Jewish converts of the descent of a cloud and the overshadowing of the Tent of Witness in the Book of Exodus. They could not have failed to think of the divine presence or *Shekinah*.

Development occurs however by mention of the same Spirit descending on Jesus at his baptism

(Mk 1:10), supporting him against Satan in the wilderness (Mk 1:12) and being present at the beginning of Jesus' ministry (Mk 4:14).

In John's Gospel the Spirit is described as the "Advocate" and "another Paraclete" or intercessor, counsellor, support and protector. He is also spoken of as the "Spirit of Truth" and as the one who would reveal and inspire true worship of God, as opposed to the devil, "the father of lies". When addressing his disciples for the last time Jesus speaks of the Holy Spirit as the One who intercedes with God the Father and who would teach the disciples.

In the Acts of the Apostles we are all familiar with how a mighty wind "filled the whole house" and how the "divine fire split into tongues and hovered over the apostles' heads" (Acts 2:1-4), and how it became one of the functions of the apostles to convey the Spirit to others by the laying on of hands (Acts 15:25).

In the writings of St Paul it is often impossible to separate the Holy Spirit from Jesus. As we have seen, for Paul the Christian life is life "in the Spirit" or life "in Christ" and very different from life "in the flesh". For him the presence of the Holy Spirit makes the Christian's body the Temple of God (1 Cor 3:16).

Most importantly, according to Paul, "the Spirit too comes to help us in our weakness. For when we cannot choose words in order to pray properly, the Spirit himself expresses our plea in a way that could never be put into words..." (Rom 8:26-27).

It is to the Holy Spirit that we are indebted for the variety of gifts and fruits that he distributes among us for a good purpose. In addition the Spirit will one day raise up our bodies as "spiritual bodies" in the likeness of Christ's resurrection (1 Cor 15:42-44).

If we wish our prayer life to be fruitful, probably the best thing possible we could do would be to call on the assistance of the Holy Spirit. As the ancient hymn says, it is after all the Holy Spirit who is capable of "washing away our squalors, watering our arid souls, bending our stubborn wills, kindling our frozen hearts and directing our straying steps."

Writing on how the Holy Spirit actualises our faith, Henri Nouwen remarks that,

> "Without Pentecost, the Christ-event – the life, death, and resurrection of Jesus – remains imprisoned in history as something simply to remember, think about, and reflect on. The Spirit of Jesus however comes to dwell within us, so that we can become living Christ here and now. Pentecost lifts the whole mystery of salvation out of its particularities and makes it something universal, embracing all peoples, all countries, all seasons and all eras. Pentecost is also the moment of empowering. Each individual human being can claim the Spirit of Jesus as the guiding spirit of his or her life. In that Spirit we can speak and act freely and confidently with the knowledge that the same Spirit that inspired Jesus is inspiring us."[3]

In our approach to God, do we sufficiently consider the place and role of the Holy Spirit in our lives as individuals and as a community? Without the acknowledged presence of the Holy Spirit in our lives, are we ever able to recognise Christ, as the two disciples finally did on the Road to Emmaus?

Points to reflect upon

1. How important is prayer to me in my daily life? What difference does it make to my life? Does my prayer life possess the signs of authenticity?
2. To what extent do I invite the Holy Spirit into my daily life?

A suggested Scriptural reading and prayer

St John, chapter 16, verses 4-15. The work of the Holy Spirit.

"O come, Holy Spirit, inflame my heart, set it on fire with love. Burn away my self-centredness so that I can love unselfishly. Breathe your life giving breath into my soul so that I can live freely and joyously, unrestricted by self-consciousness, and may be ready to go wherever you may send me. Come like a gentle breeze and give me your still peace so that I may be quiet and know the wonder of your presence, and help diffuse it in the world. Never let me shut you out; never let me try to limit you to my capacity; act freely in me and through me, never leave me, O Lord and giver of life."

Michael Hollings and Eta Gullick
in *The Oxford Book of Prayer*

Practical Suggestions

1. Through prayer invite the Holy Spirit into your daily life.
2. Discover the particular gifts we may receive from the Holy Spirit.

NOTES

1. John Chapman, *Spiritual Letters*, p.80, edited by Dom Roger Huddeston (first pub. 1935) New Ark Library. Quoted in David Forrester, *Listening with the Heart,* Burns and Oates, 1978, pp.62-63.
2. *De Trinitate*, Bk 3, ch 19.
3. Henri Nouwen, *Jesus a Gospel*, Orbis Books, 2001, pp.131-132.

Chapter 7

The Meaning of Community

"He cannot have God for his father who has not the Church for his mother."　　　　(Cyprian)

In 1973 a newly qualified professional Counsellor, who happened to be a Christian, was asked by the Mother Superior of a convent to address her nuns, most of whom were working among adolescents in care, on the concept of community living that he had been taught in his training. He agreed to do so, but shortly afterwards was contacted by the Superior once again with the news that several of the nuns had objected. They were adamant that the Counsellor, not being the member of a religious order and, as it happened, single, would have no real experience of what it meant to live in community. The Mother Superior assured him that she personally hoped that he would come, but warned him that he might receive a hostile reception from some of the sisters at question time. The Counsellor thought carefully and then said that he would still like to come.

On the day in question he stood in front of the nuns, who numbered about fifty, and began by saying that before he started his talk he would like to speak about something personal, namely his family background. Despite being single, he wanted to assure them that he knew quite a lot about family life, being the product of a marriage and having watched his parents' marriage at close quarters from the "inside", which is surely the first experience most of us have of community living.

He told the nuns that his father had been a permanent invalid as a result of having been wounded and gassed in the First World War. His mother had run away from home as a young woman in order to become a nurse; an action precipitated by her parents being Victorian in outlook and believing that a woman's place was in the home. When she felt compelled to leave without a word, her parents disowned her.

It was in the hospital where she first obtained her training and was later employed that she and the Counsellor's father first met. She was the nursing Sister in charge of his ward when he was repatriated from France for medical treatment to his wounds. They fell in love and married.

The Counsellor informed the nuns that, as a result, he later learned a great deal about how sickness could affect a marriage, how a woman being the bread-winner could alter the balance in such a marriage, and how animosity between relatives in a family, such as that felt between his mother and her parents, could poison the atmosphere within a family community.

Then he explained how first his brother was born and afterwards himself and how in the depression of the 1930s poverty became a considerable factor within the family, affecting the food they were able to buy, the clothes they wore and how they paid household bills.

None of this however prevented his mother showing them the importance of prayer by kneeling every night by her bed and saying her prayers, no matter how busy her day as now a district nurse had been, teaching both of them their catechism, and escorting them to church each Sunday.

When the Second World War broke out, with evacuees arriving and the blitz and rationing beginning, he described how community life, in both his family and the neighbourhood was drastically affected by requiring them to share their material lives with the evacuees.

In the last year of the war his brother along with several of his friends was killed on active service, so he then witnessed how death and bereavement brought sadness into a family, the neighbourhood, and wider community.

His mother, deeply distressed by his brother's death, was soon afterwards involved in a car crash involving her being in intensive care for several weeks. It was at this point that he explained that, as a consequence, he had learnt a great deal about the effects of trauma within a community.

He went on to tell the nuns how his father contracted cancer at the age of sixty and required constant nursing for three years before his death. Afterwards his mother then lived on to the age of ninety-two, so he knew quite a bit about caring for the elderly at home and within a community.

Finally, he asked the nuns whether there was anyone among them who now considered that he knew nothing about community life as lived out in a family and neighbourhood, whether one was talking of what today we call a nuclear family or an extended one. No one spoke up.

The fact is one cannot be a human being and especially a Christian without being part of a community. As the poet John Donne said, "No man is an island." This is especially true when it comes to worship. The writer, Ronald Rolheiser says, "For a Christian concrete involvement within an historical community of faith (church going) is a non-negotiable within the spiritual life" (*Seeking Spirituality*). He acknowledges that this concept is a difficult one for our age, which increasingly believes in God but is disillusioned with the institutional church. The notion of community however is not only vital in terms of worship.

What we call the 'Body of Christ' is not just the historical Jesus who walked the earth 2,000 years ago, and not only the Real Presence in the Blessed Sacrament, but also the body of believers on earth. Indeed St John Chrysostom was of the view that Christians are joined to one another and to Christ "like flour in a loaf." Furthermore, as St John tells us in his First Epistle, it is these, with all their faults and failings, that we are commanded to love.

> "Anyone who says, 'I love God', and hates his brother is a liar, since a man who does not love the brother that he can see cannot love God, whom he has never seen." (1 Jn 4:20)

Our faith, however much we might prefer it otherwise, is not an individualistic thing. It has a communal dimension. We are not simply social animals either, but bound by what Jesus commanded. When the lawyer in St Luke's Gospel (10:25-28.) asked what he should do to inherit eternal life, Jesus asked him, "What is written in the Law? What do you read there?" The lawyer replied: "You must love the Lord your God with all your heart, with all your soul, with all your strength, and with all your mind, and your neighbour as yourself." To which Jesus replied, "You have answered right, do this and life is yours." (cf Mt 22:34-40)

When the lawyer, who we are told was anxious to justify himself, then asked Jesus, "And who is my neighbour?" Jesus responded with the parable of the Good Samaritan telling the lawyer to go and show pity like the Good Samaritan. (Lk 10:37)

The concept of being related to others and obliged to love others is essential for a Christian. It is this concept of being part of a body greater than ourselves that is at the root of the idea of community. It is linked to the fact that we are all made in God's image. That is what makes our neighbour valuable with rights. It is further based on St John's words, all found in his First Letter.

> "We can be sure," he writes, "that we are in God only when the one who claims to be living in him is living the same kind of life as Christ lived."

> "My children, our love is not to be just words or mere talk, but something real and active; only by this can we be certain that we are children of the truth…"

> "His (God's) commandments are these: that we believe in the name of his Son Jesus Christ and that we love one another."

> "Anyone who fails to love can never have known God…"

> "My dear people, since God has loved us so much, we too should love one another."

"As long as we love one another God will live in us."

All these words are applicable to every Christian community at all times whether we are referring to our family, parish, neighbourhood or Church.

In 1979 Jean Vanier first published his book *Community and Growth* which was later revised. And although this seems a long time ago now, it remains impressive, with valuable things to teach us. In the book Vanier describes different essential aspects of community living.

He first writes of *Community as Belonging* and speaks movingly about the differences concerning community between the countries of the developing world and the western world, especially Africa. He quotes a wonderful story of how if a prize is offered for the first to answer a question in a group of Canadian Indian children, they all work out the answer together and shout it out at the same time as they couldn't bear to win, leaving the rest as losers. Further in this section Vanier writes that those in community should be a springboard towards all humanity. "I cannot be," he says, "a universal brother or sister unless I first love my people."

Next he describes community as *openness*. Vanier says that "The difference between community and a group of friends is that in a community we verbalise our mutual belonging and bonding." It is pertinent that he quotes Esther de Waal when she writes of religious life in a monastery and says:

"It is noticeable how both the abbot and the cellarer are constantly concerned about the brethren, caring for each singly in all their uniqueness rather than with the community en bloc, that ideal which seems to haunt so much contemporary ideology. The common life [she continues] never becomes a piece of abstract idealisation or idealism. St Benedict would probably have appreciated Dietrich Bonhoeffer's aphorism: 'He who loves community, destroys community; he who loves the brethren, builds community.'"

This idea continues in Vanier's next section dealing with community as *caring*. Here he remarks that "Community must never take precedence over individual people. It is for people and for their growth."

"If community is for the growth of the personal consciousness," he continues, "with the security it brings, there will be times when some people find themselves in conflict with their community."

He analyses this and concludes that "the authenticity of their communion with God is shown as they continually try to love their brothers and sisters with greater fidelity, without judgement or condemnation." Vanier goes on to say that community is a place of communion where the brethren become vulnerable to one another and then moves on to community and co-operation. He argues that, "In community, collaboration must find its source in communion... Co-operation without communion," he says, "quickly becomes like a work camp or factory... When a community is just a place of work, it is in danger of dying."

His next description is community as *a place of healing and growth*. He says that after what we would call the honeymoon period, community can be a terrible place, because he says, it is a place of relationships (as distinct from when one lives alone). Finally Vanier writes of community as *forgiveness.*

It is obviously no easy task either simply being a member of any kind of community – family, parish, neighbourhood, village or town and so on – or loving one's brethren! When it comes to the Church as community, it can be just as hard, if not harder.

This is made clear in Carlo Carretto's book *I Sought and I Found* (1984), in which Carretto writes of both his love and exasperation with the Church.

> "How much I criticize you, my community and yet how much I love you!
> You have made me suffer more than anyone and yet I owe more to you than to anyone.
> (There are times when) I should like to see you destroyed and yet I need your presence.
> You have given me much scandal and yet you alone have made me understand holiness.
> Never in this world have I seen anything more compromised, more false, yet never have I touched anything more pure, more generous or more beautiful.
> Countless times I have felt like slamming the door of my soul in your face – and yet, every night, I have prayed that I might die in your sure arms!
> No, I cannot be free of you, for I am one with you, even if not completely you.
> Then too – where should I go?

To build another community?
But I could not build one without the same defects, for they are my defects.
And again, if I were to build another community, it would be my community, not Christ's community.
No, I am old enough. I know better!"

Ronald Rolheiser in his book, *Seeking Spirituality*, spends a whole section describing spiritual images of the Church, and explaining how the Church is not just a gathering of like-minded individuals, a group who huddle in fear or loneliness, a family in the psychological sense, people who share a common roof and denomination and even simply a common mission, although these are all ways some people look at community. Rolheiser tells a fascinating story of how a young man once joined the Oblates (Rolheiser's own Order).

He describes the young man as very idealistic but emotionally needy. Time and time again at community meetings he complained about lack of community, saying such things as: 'I joined this order, looking for community, but everyone is always too busy to have time for me. We don't share deeply enough with each other. There is no real intimacy among us. We are too cold, too masculine. I'm forever lonely and nobody much cares!'

Rolheiser says, the young man was right about the community. No religious community is perfect, but that was not his problem – false expectations were. Eventually the young man went for counselling and at one point the counsellor, a priest-psychologist who understood the dynamics of community life, told him: ' What you are looking for is not to be found in a religious order. You are looking for a lover, not a religious order.'

Too often we regard community as a substitute for what it is not intended to be. People are notorious for complaining about what is lacking in their community whether it be their extended family, parish community, neighbourhood, diocese or Church, but how accurate is our understanding of community? Christian communal life, in whatever context one is considering it, can only prosper if its purpose is more than for itself, its vision more than looking inwards, and if efficiency is balanced with charity for all.

A picture of the ideal Christian community is contained in the fourth chapter of *The Acts of the Apostles*, verses 32 to 35.

> "The whole group of believers was united, heart and soul; no one claimed for his own use anything that he had, as everything they owned was held in common. The apostles continued to testify to the resurrection of the Lord Jesus with great power, and they were all given great respect. None of their members was ever in want, as all those who owned land or houses would sell them, and bring the money from them, to present it to the apostles; it was then distributed to any members who might be in need."

Even so this first Christian community and the early Church which followed were not without their internal problems, especially that of heresy and combating it. Perhaps the first and truly great theologian of the Church, Irenaeus of Lyons (c.130–c.200), devoted a massive work, *Against Heresies*, to defending the faith from error. He had the insight too to grasp that the real danger of those who are opposed to the truth is not their hostility, but their ability to assimilate their ideas to it. This tendency is an ever present danger within any community. Often we are the first to judge and blame our neighbour believing that we are in the right, forgetting Jesus' words,

> "Do not judge, and you will not be judged; because the judgements you give are the judgements you will get, and the amount you measure out is the amount you will be given. Why," he asks, "do you observe the splinter in your brother's eye and never notice the plank in your own? How dare you say to your brother, 'Let me take the splinter out of your eye', when all the time there is a plank in your own? Hypocrite! Take the plank out of your own eye first, and then you will see clearly enough to take the splinter out of your brother's eye."
>
> (Mt 7:1-5)

This was made clear to a teacher some years ago when he received an urgent and totally unexpected letter from one of his closest friends. They had trained together in college many years before. This friend was living in the North of England. He wrote saying he was dying and had been told that he had only three months to live. (It turned out that he had just a month.)

The following morning the recipient of the letter got up at 5 a.m. and caught the first train to Edinburgh and the north. As he sat on the train his mind was totally distracted. It was full of thoughts and memories. After all, he and his friend had known each other for thirty-seven years. He was worried as to what he would find on his arrival. He was also worried as to how he would cope with the death of his friend. He wondered if his Christian faith would uphold him.

He was so preoccupied that he didn't notice the train stop at a particular station, but he couldn't help noticing the two large people, clearly a husband and wife, who then came into the railway carriage. They struggled to get into their seats which were immediately opposite him.

No sooner had the train started than the woman reached into her bag and pulled out a large Danish pastry. She proceeded without pausing to demolish it. The teacher had no choice but to sit, watch and listen to this happening. Then she dipped into her bag again and took out a large bottle of coca cola, held it to her lips and polished that off. Meanwhile the husband went off to a different part of the train for a cigarette. To escape, the teacher closed his eyes. When he ventured to open his eyes again, the woman was staring at him. He felt distinctly uncomfortable! It had to be he she was staring at, there was no one behind him.

"I didn't want to make this journey, you know", she said.

"Excuse me?" he said, somewhat surprised.

"We're off to see my mother," she said. "I hate my mother", she added with emphasis.

"The only consolation is that she hates my husband more than she hates me!"

By now the teacher felt trapped in a nightmare.

"We deliberately live in the south," she went on, "because she lives in the north."

"She has reduced my dad to an invalid and has alienated everyone else – family and neighbours. She has no friends. I hate her!" she repeated.

Then she went on, "I am an only child and I don't remember a time when she didn't make my life hell." By now the teacher wondered why she was dumping all this on him, a complete stranger? Furthermore she was not a child, but a woman in her fifties. What is going on, he asked himself?

He then ventured a question, "May I say something?"

She nodded.

"How will you feel when your mother dies?" he asked.

"Won't you regret all you are now saying? And won't it then be too late to be reconciled?"

"Do you know", he continued, "I have met lots of people who, after someone has died, say, 'Oh, why didn't I say this or do that', but then it's too late and consequently they are loaded with guilt."

"I can only think of today not the future", she replied. And then fell silent.

She didn't speak again and he never did discover who she was.

He is still wondering what has happened to her. He hopes that one day she can let go of her hate. Hate is an ugly emotion. And it makes those who engage in hate ugly people.

Failing to love a fellow member of the Christian community is another thing which prevents us recognising Christ as we journey through life. Often it is our tongue which causes us to fail in love.

Suggested questions to consider

1. To what extent are we sometimes guilty of judging and speaking uncharitably of our neighbour, forgetting that they are members of our community? Is this important?

2. After attending church on a Sunday, do we make a conscious effort to speak to other worshippers, especially the handicapped and elderly?

3. How do we regard the Sign of Peace at Mass and do we mind exchanging it with our fellow worshippers?

Suggested Scriptural reading

Acts chapter 4, verses 32-37. The Early Church.
Philippians chapter 2, verses 14-15. Paul's advice on how Christians should behave.

Practical suggestions

1. Consider what measures – no matter how small – you could take to build up a sense of community within your parish.

2. Encourage in some practical way the young people of your parish to feel that they are active members of a community, such as by supporting a parish youth club, or organising a parish retreat or pilgrimage specifically geared to their needs.

Chapter 8

The Breaking of Bread

"Now while he (Jesus) was with them at table, he took bread and said the blessing; then he broke it and handed it to them. And their eyes were opened and they recognised him; but he had vanished from their sight. Then they said to each other, 'Did not our hearts burn within us as he talked on the road and explained the Scriptures to us?'" (Lk 24:31-32)

Food and shelter are basic essentials for everyone. After completing their journey to Emmaus the two disciples were eager to share both with Jesus, who as yet they had failed to recognise but who had accompanied them on the road. Their offering of hospitality to a fellow traveller is usually put down to the fact that his words had had such a powerful effect on them. ("Did not our hearts burn within us…?") This is surely true, but their gesture also has something vital to say to those of us who live in the twenty-first century. Are we for example as concerned as much as we should be for the basic needs of those who live in the developing countries, especially Africa?

In our world today, by the time the present generation of school children has grown up, the world will be smaller not in size but in what everyone in the affluent world at least has in common. Already we eat similar foods. If we were to examine the shelves of any supermarket, it's amazing how many of the different types of fruit are available, not necessarily in season in the countries where they are being sold, such as avocados from Israel, cherries from Argentina, kiwi from New Zealand and grapes from South Africa. This is not to mention other types of food. Everywhere too there are such coffee houses as Starbucks and Costa and eating houses such as Pizza Hut and Kentucky Fried Chicken. By 1997 Macdonald's, founded in 1955, had built 22,000 restaurants in more than a hundred countries. They are to be found in such diverse cities as Moscow, La Paz, Paris and Hong Kong and serve more than 40 million customers daily.

Where there are cars they all need oil from the Middle East, Texas, the North Sea and Nigeria, so when world oil prices rise so do prices at our local petrol pumps. Everyday more and more people in the developed world are in touch through the use of mobile phones, telephone and video conferences, e-mails and faxes or combinations of them. On television we watch many of the same programmes. *Friends* for example can be seen in Los Angeles and Delhi, *The Simpsons* in Manchester and Toronto, *Neighbours* in Croydon and Sydney, not to mention films produced in Hollywood. Similarly and most importantly news is flashed around the world at great speed. It is as Marshall McLuhan said as early as 1962, "The electronic age has sealed the entire human family into a single global tribe."

In terms of trade and laws the world is getting smaller already. Twenty-five countries are joined together in the European Union; the USA, Canada and Mexico are linked in trade agreements; and there is a rapidly expanding net work of trade between the

People's Republic of China, Singapore and other Chinese speaking countries in Asia.

People themselves are on the move as never before. The majority, but not all, are moving from the developing world to the Western world. Some are asylum seekers, but many are economic migrants, seeking a higher standard of living. In 2005 the United Nations estimated that 191 million immigrants or 3% of the world's population were on the move from countries in which they were originally born.

London sums up what is happening. In a population of 7.1 million only 4.3 million are British. The remainder comprise Asians, Africans, people from the Caribbean, those of mixed race, as well as Arabs, Americans, Australians and Eastern Europeans to mention just a few. London has become the most cosmopolitan and amazing city in the world. Its streets are loud with exotic languages (in total 300 different languages) and bright with Muslim veils and beards, African robes and Caribbean dreadlocks. All of which gives the impression that the people of the world are getting closer. But beneath the surface there are problems that will not go away.

Bill Clinton, the former American President, has described the steady growth of globalisation as leading to "a world without walls", and Tony Blair when Prime Minister of the United Kingdom spoke of this process as "inevitable and irresistible." And although there is an inexorable integration of markets, nation states and technologies to an extent and at a speed never seen before, it can be argued that the poorer countries suffer disproportionately whenever there is a down turn in the material prosperity of the first world nations. Whereas the nations comprising the

G8 (now rapidly tending to be overshadowed by the G20 nations), consisting of Canada, France, Germany, Italy, Japan, Russia, the United Kingdom and the USA represent just 14% of the world's population, they are responsible for 65% of the world's economy measured by gross domestic product.

Furthermore, globalisation may be a world-wide drive towards a global economic system, but it is dominated by multi-national corporations and banking institutions that are not accountable to democratic processes or national governments. Whereas globalisation reduces the power of governments to determine their policies and destinies, the stock market has a global effect. What occurs on Wall Street or the London stock exchange has repercussions around the world.

It is questionable too whether multinationals benefit the poorer countries. They account for over 33% of world output and 66% of world trade and there are at least 500 of them, but none are owned by countries in the developing world. One quarter of world trade occurs between multinationals, but they are notorious for employing people in the developing world, in a process known as out-sourcing, on wages considerably lower than in the West. Among other things multi-nationals also seek to create new needs, such as the use of tobacco in the less affluent counties. They also exploit the teenage market in the West, especially when it comes to fashion and food, and youth is essentially prized for its spending power.

We may speak cosily of living in a "global village", but the reality is that the gap between rich and poor has widened as globalisation has accelerated. As David Landes, the retired Professor of economics and history at Harvard, has observed, the difference in income per head between the richest nation (Switzerland) and the poorest non-industrial nation (Mozambique) is 400 to 1. He reckons that two hundred and fifty years ago the gap between the richest and poorest was probably 5 to 1 and between Europe and China and India 2 to 1. Today China and India have the education, technology and resources to close the gap between them and the advanced industrial nations, but Africa is a different story. The number of people in poverty in Africa has doubled in the past two decades. Africa was left by its colonial legacy with neither the education nor the resources to take advantage of the new technology.

It is true that globalisation encourages integration on a world wide scale in ways other than economic, for example in politics, sport, law, public health, and religion and therefore in itself is not necessarily a bad thing. It is how it works that is bad. It lacks an ethical dimension and proper organisation to benefit all peoples, which for the Christian is a matter of vital importance.[1] The existence of poverty in the developing world is highly relevant to Jesus' commandment that we should love our neighbour. The sharing of good fortune with others is a *sine qua non* for a Christian and it was in the "breaking of bread" with Jesus that the two disciples at Emmaus finally recognised Jesus.

On every Sabbath devout Jews celebrate an evening family meal with prayers and readings from the Scriptures. Ever since their escape from slavery in Egypt the Jewish people have also always commemorated this event with a Passover meal. Converts from Judaism to Christianity in the early Church would have been reminded of this when reading in St Matthew's Gospel the story of Jesus feeding the five thousand. This is not just a simple story, it is one full of symbols and meaning. It is a story with something to teach us.

In Matthew's Gospel Jesus twice feeds large crowds. In chapter 14 he feeds five thousand men, not to mention the number of women and children, and does so by taking five loaves and two fish, and, in the traditional manner at every Jewish meal, first raises his eyes to heaven, blesses them, breaks them, and hands them to his disciples to be distributed to the crowd. Here Matthew is anticipating what will occur at the Last Supper. The twelve baskets of left-over scraps also represent the twelve tribes of Israel, here served by Jesus' twelve disciples. The whole miracle story deliberately echoes the story in the Old Testament of the miraculous feeding of the people of Israel, when Moses was leading them through the desert from Egypt to the Promised Land, only here Jesus is the new Moses. It echoes the occasion when God fed the people of Israel with manna and quails. It also anticipates the other long held Jewish idea of a banquet which will occur at the end of time when Jesus the Messiah returns and inaugurates the kingdom of heaven (Isa 25, 55 and Lk 22:15-20).

According to the gospel narratives Jesus appeared to his disciples a number of times after his death and resurrection, but even after his ascension and the cessation of the appearances the disciples continued to gather for their weekly meal of fellowship. The difference now however was that, when they shared the bread and passed the cup, they did so not simply as devout Jews but in memory of Jesus. In other words they were following the instructions which Jesus had given at the Last Supper and in the earliest record of this, (1 Cor 11:23-27, written around the year AD 57): it was believed that for those present the cup that they shared was a communion with the blood of Christ and the bread that they broke was a communion with the body of Christ. Moreover, because the Lord's Supper commemorated Jesus' death as well as his resurrection and, because it bore a likeness to a Passover meal, participants were able to compare the slaying of Jesus with the sacrifice of the paschal lamb. What gradually followed over the process of time was the evolution of a communal type of worship or sacrament, known as the Eucharist, meaning Thanksgiving, involving prayer, readings from Scripture, a homily, the consecration of bread and wine, followed by holy communion.

Today, according to Pope Benedict XVI,

"The Eucharist makes the Risen Christ constantly present, Christ who continues to give himself to us, calling us to participate in the banquet of his Body and Blood. From this full communion with him comes every other element of the life of the Church, in the first place the communion among the faithful, the commitment to proclaim and give witness to the Gospel, the ardour of charity towards all, especially toward the poor and the smallest."

(*Let God's Light Shine Forth*)

Points for reflection

1. How important for us is it that we should regularly receive Holy Communion?
2. Has our understanding of the Eucharist developed since we were children?

Suggested Scriptural reading

1 Corinthians 11:23-27. An early account of the Lord's Supper handed down to St Paul.

Practical suggestions

1. If possible try to support more the work of such charities in the developing world such as CAFOD.
2. If they exist in your parish, have you considered offering yourself as a Special Minister in order to take Holy Communion to the sick and housebound?

NOTE

1. Pope Benedict XVI, *Caritas in Veritate*, (2009).

Chapter 9

Finding God in the Scriptures

"Then, starting with Moses and going through all the prophets, he (Jesus) explained to them the passages throughout the Scriptures that were about himself." (Lk 24.27)

In the mind of a Christian the word revelation, when spoken of in connection with both the Old and New Testaments of the Bible, refers to the self-disclosure of the God of mercy and love. Among other things it informs us of his plan of salvation to rescue us from oppression, sin, sickness and death; all the results of our having disobeyed him. According to the Second Vatican Council document, *Dei Verbum*, God is the author of Sacred Scripture.

> "The divinely revealed realities, which are contained and presented in the text of Sacred Scripture, have been written down under the inspiration of the Holy Spirit."[1]

This nevertheless does not mean that a reader of the Bible must ignore the fact that those who wrote what God wished them to write were influenced by the conditions of their time and culture, the different types of literature they were used to, and the various ways in which writers expressed what they had to say. This accounts for the existence within the Bible of different forms of literature, ranging from the historical and prophetic to the poetic. Ultimately it is the Church which is the judge of how Scripture should be interpreted.[2] Together with Tradition, Scripture is part of the two-fold source of revelation or of what God has disclosed to us, which climaxes in the Person and teaching of Jesus.

The Bible also illustrates not only how God put his plan of salvation into operation, but how he makes us his own in a special way. In order to learn how we may find God, understand him more deeply, and draw close to him, we surely need to make part of our daily prayerful reading at least those sections of the Bible referring to this?

In the beginning we are told how God made himself known to our first parents, not merely through the evidence and beauty of his creation, with which the Bible begins, but by conversing with them, as illustrated in the Book of Genesis. Even after what is known as the Fall or the failure of the human race to obey God's commandments and their pursuit of their own selfish ends, God did not abandon them. Instead, and in the face of continual examples of men and women choosing to abuse their free will and engage in polytheism and idolatry, God embarked on his plan of salvation or rescue. According to St Paul (Eph 1:9-10) God had such a plan from all eternity, which would climax with the advent of his Son, Jesus, into our world.

First God offered a covenant with Noah for mankind, vowing never again to annihilate his creation on account of the sins of the human race. This covenant remained in force until the coming of Jesus, despite the continuance of human self indulgence and presumption.

Then, in order still to form a moral human society, God makes another attempt to persuade humankind to fall in with his expectations, only this time concentrating on and choosing the family of one man, Abraham. The story of Abraham and thus, through his descendants, Israel, is one of a chosen people being moulded and shaped by God down the centuries through exile, slavery and suffering. His purpose was to form a people who would one day be the root on to which all people would be grafted.

After the era of the Patriarchs, beginning with Abraham, God freed the people of Israel under the leadership of Moses from slavery in Egypt and established a covenant with them on Mount Sinai, giving them his law. The process of forming his chosen people was continued by God through the work of the prophets; a process which gave the tribes of Israel the expectation of a new and eternal covenant, only this time to be written on their hearts.[3] This hope was something which, in a sense, occurred most in the lives of the *anawim*, mentioned in an earlier chapter.

Ultimately, the plan of salvation and the process of God revealing himself, culminated in the incarnation of Jesus, God's Son, in whom God established his covenant for ever.[4] Understanding of this throws considerable light on the reason why St Jerome could say that "Ignorance of Scripture is ignorance of Christ".

How we picture Jesus

In a most thought provoking book, entitled *Moral Wisdom*, the Jesuit James F. Keenan, has a chapter on Jesus in the New Testament. He begins by telling the story of how he once led a day of recollection for twelve nuns working in Rome. He says that all of them, except one, were animated, charitable or hospitable. The exception was the oldest, the most off-putting and clearly the most sad.

He began the day by asking each of them to describe how they imagined God to be, what was their idea of him, and how they prayed to him. One nun who worked as the headmistress of a school replied that she thought of Jesus chiefly as a teacher. Another who worked in a hospital said that she imagined Jesus as a healer. A third who was charismatically inclined spoke of praying to the Holy Spirit. All this appeared perfectly understandable. There seemed nothing untoward about all this, until he enquired of the unhappy nun how she thought of God and received the answer that she prayed to the Baby Jesus. At this the eleven other nuns and the priest were astonished.

Trying not to sound rude, the priest then asked the sad nun what God said in response.

"Babies can't talk!" came the quick retort.

"So what does he do?" asked the priest.

"Burp" came the reply.

"What do you do?" he then inquired.

The nun replied that she patted the Baby Jesus, changed his nappies and things like that.

"Is there anyone else who comes into your prayer?" asked the priest.

"Well, I let people visit him, but after some time I send them away and I put him to bed" answered the nun.

For eighty years this unhappy nun had been praying to a baby.

Clearly we all tend to picture God in ways that we find most comfortable, that we can relate to most easily and which do not disturb us. But doesn't this tell us more about ourselves than about God? Furthermore, aren't all the ways in which we imagine God inadequate? And to a degree aren't we all guilty of tailoring the idea or picture we might have to suit our own needs?

Each of the Gospel writers present us with a particular image of Jesus, according to the audience they were initially addressing, their own background and own idea or experience of Jesus. Listening to the words and preaching of St Peter in Rome, Mark for example, would have been influenced as his interpreter by what the leader of the apostles had to say. The picture of Jesus in St Matthew's Gospel, probably first written in Aramaic in Palestine, was especially suited to Jewish converts. The picture of Jesus we derive from St Luke's Gospel was assuredly affected by the author's own pagan origins and his considerable understanding of St Paul, whom he accompanied on the latter's second and third missionary journeys and two Roman captivities. The Gospel of St John is especially concerned to proclaim Jesus as Messiah and Son of God and is specifically aimed at enabling us to believe in the Messiah.

Regardless then of our personal preferences in our picturing of Jesus and the way in which we may pray to him, it surely makes sense to try to embrace each of the Gospel images in turn. As was pointed out in chapter one, no one way of describing God can do him justice and it is precisely the same when we attempt to picture Jesus, his Son. No one image is sufficient to describe him adequately or completely.

Jesus himself resorted to a variety of metaphors when speaking of himself, as when he described himself as the Bread of Life (Jn 6:35,49), the

Light of the World (Jn 7:12), the Good Shepherd (Jn 10:11), and not least in his farewell discourses to his disciples, where he described himself as the Way, the Truth and the Life (Jn 14:6), the True Vine, (Jn 15:1) and elsewhere as the Son of Man, (Mt 13:24-27 and Lk 17:22-30).

The more we acquaint ourselves with these metaphors and ponder their meaning, the more fruitful will our journey on our particular road through life become.

Point for reflection

How well do we know from Scripture the history of God's plan of salvation for us and the ways it affects us?

Suggested Scriptural reading

St John's Gospel, chapter 15, verses 1-17. Jesus the True Vine.

Practical suggestions

Determine to include a reading from the Gospels each day, no matter how briefly or how tired we may be.

NOTES

1. The Second Vatican Council, *Dei Verbum* 11.
2. *Ibid* 12:3.
3. See Isaiah 2:2-4; Jeremiah 31: 31-34; Hebrews 10:16.
4. See Hebrews 1:1-2.

Chapter 10

Sin as a Hindrance to Finding God

"Just as water extinguishes a fire, so love wipes away sin."　　　　　　　　　　(John of God)

Imagine the reaction today if an Israeli on his way from Jerusalem to Jericho were to be set upon, beaten up and abandoned by a gang of robbers and a Palestinian assisted him to recover. Of course the scenario might be that of a Palestinian being set upon and an Israeli coming to his defence.

Another situation might be that of a Christian in the Middle East in similar circumstances being rescued by a Muslim, or, not so long ago, a Catholic in Northern Ireland coming to help a Protestant or vice versa. Such actions would merit headline coverage in the press.

In order to emphasise that love knows no racial, social, ethnic or religious boundaries, in St Luke's Gospel (Lk 10:30-37) Jesus tells the parable of the Good Samaritan. In this both a priest and a Levite, who might have been expected to come to the aid of a victim of robbers, chose to ignore the situation. They passed by on the other side. On the other hand, a Samaritan, who generally speaking might have regarded the victim as no friend, came to the rescue.

Today we increasingly encounter in the press or on television, as well as in daily life, instances of prejudice and discrimination, even persecution. We still have not taken on board the lesson of the parable of the Good Samaritan that love overrides all differences of colour, race or creed. What is more important than all of these differences is the common humanity we all share, together with the important fact that sin is basically a failure to love.

Harmatia

In an earlier work, entitled *I Know Their Sorrows*, I attempted to describe the essence of sin. There I wrote of sin as a form of blindness, of Jesus' mission as one of freeing mankind from its thraldom to sin, of the Pharisees' obsession with Law, how sin entered our world, how a solely mechanical and individualistic concept of sin robs it of its real existential meaning and so on. I also mentioned how in the New Testament the most commonly used word for sin is *harmatia*, derived from the idea of shooting and missing or falling short of a target. This interpretation is in-valuable in understanding the role of so many of the people in Jesus' parables. It explains the sinfulness for instance of the priest and Levite in the parable of the Good Samaritan, that of the rich man, who neglected Lazarus, the beggar at his gate, and the son who failed to go into the field to work as he said he would, to mention just three examples. All of them failed in one way or another to consider the needs of others, in other words to love.

Failure to love and therefore failure to keep the commandment to love God and our neighbour does not have to be dramatic or outstanding to prevent us from finding God in our lives. Murder, lying, cheating, stealing, slander and adultery have always been regarded as grave sins by the Church. Failure to love is more frequently found in most of us in our adoption of a complacent attitude not only towards God but towards other people. This occurs most often when we take the latter for granted, fail to express our appreciation of them, ignore them, or are simply being insensitive to their needs. The frequency of this type of sin, as distinct from any graver forms, is such that after a while we lose even our awareness of our failure to love.

The truth is it is so easy to become complacent in our relations with God. Too often we take God for granted and fail not only to understand our creaturely situation in relation to him, but how greatly God loves us and showed the extent of his love by sending us Jesus.

If we examine our behaviour towards those we love in our own family it is often the same as how we behave towards God. Our failure to pray may be compared to our failing, through laziness or sulking, to speak to someone in the family that we deeply love and who loves us. There may even be occasions when people of all ages within a family, young and old, might deny they were being self-centred but, through obstinacy, might simply be bent on so-called enjoying themselves, no matter how this might affect others.

This selfishness is often most evident in the many instances when we fail to love others outside our families, in the sense of failing to will their good. Too often we regard others as means to suit our own ends. We might desire them for their looks, envy them their good fortune, attempt to ingratiate ourselves with them because of their position or influence, use them as stepping stones for our own advancement, flatter them in order to win their approval and so on. All of these are occasions of a failure to love in the sense of our not genuinely regarding them as human beings with rights and wanting their good. All of them are also types of behaviour which are sinful and therefore alien to enabling us both to find and draw close to God on our journey.

Conversion

It is not unusual for us to become inured to our own sinfulness, to make excuses for our wrongful behaviour, and gradually not to recognise our failure to love God and our neighbour. It is precisely then that we need a change of heart or what is called in Greek, *metanoia,* the term for conversion.

Down through the centuries Christianity has given instances of individuals who have come to recognise their sinfulness and experienced a conversion to the Gospel. In the New Testament there are such examples as Mary Magdalene, the Ethiopian eunuch, the centurion Cornelius, and not least St Paul on his road to Damascus. In the early Church perhaps the most well known conversion was that of Augustine of Hippo, in the Middle Ages one thinks of Thomas Becket and Francis of Assisi, and in the sixteenth century, Ignatius Loyola and Philip Neri. Perhaps the most famous conversion in the new world in the seventeenth century was that of Pocahontas, the daughter of an American Indian chief, who married the Virginian colonist, John Rolfe, in 1614 and died during a visit to England two years later.

In the eighteenth century more than a few Evangelical Christians in England were famous for undergoing conversion to Christ and changing their ways of behaviour. Some like John Wesley experienced it in a dramatic way and could pin point it precisely. In his journal, Wesley notes that, at 8.45 p.m. on

14 May 1738, he felt "my heart strangely warmed. I felt I did trust in Christ, Christ alone, for salvation; and an assurance was given me, that he had taken *my* sins, even *mine*, and saved me from the law of sin and death."[1]

The conversion of such as William Huntington, who in his youth led a thoroughly dissolute life, was equally powerful. He says that one day he became intensely conscious of sin and that, "I leapt up, with my eyes ready to start out of my head, my hair standing erect, and my countenance stained with all the horrible gloom and dismay of the damned." He subsequently received a vision of the Holy Spirit and "heard a voice from heaven, saying unto me in plain words, 'Lay by your forms of prayers, and go pray to Jesus Christ; do you not see how pitifully he speaks to Sinners.'"[2]

Not all conversions in the eighteenth and nineteenth centuries were dramatic, but all resulted in a change of heart and behaviour in the recipients. Among their number were the hymn writer John Berridge, the poet William Cowper, the theologian, John Fletcher, the former slave trader, John Newton, the famous politician, William Wilberforce, the future Catholic Cardinal, John Henry Newman, to name just a few. In modern times, it is Thomas Merton, the Cistercian monk, who before his conversion to Christianity led what can only be called a pagan existence, who is probably best known for having undergone a conversion experience.

Whatever form conversion takes, it involves awakening to the need to change our ways, to be more serious about loving God and our neighbour, and to deepen our relationship with Christ in many of the different ways described in earlier chapters. The truth is most of us need this *metanoia* experience in order that we should not become complacent.

For many of us sin is a form of blindness to our failure to love. The disciples on the Road to Emmaus were in a sense blind to the fact that the stranger among them was Jesus. Were they too caught up in their own personal situation to realise his presence? On our journey we must by contrast keep our eyes open to our weaknesses and failures and not become obsessed with ourselves.

Suggested points for reflection

1. Do we recognise the work of Jesus in our lives?
2. To what extent are we in need of a conversion to enable us to draw closer to Jesus?

A suggested Scriptural reading

Acts chapter 9, verses 1-18. The Conversion of Paul.

Practical suggestion

Make a thorough Examination of Conscience, beginning with how we may have neglected to thank God for the good things in our lives, how we have failed to seek his forgiveness for the times we have sinned against others, and when we have let ourselves down by giving in to such temptations as greed, anger, lack of charity, laziness and pride.

NOTES
1. John Wesley, *Journal*, Vol.1, p.51.
2. W. Huntington, *The Kingdom of God taken by Prayer*, first pub. 1770, available in paperback 1966.

Chapter 11

Conclusion

"Often fill your mind with thoughts of the great gentleness and mercy with which God our Saviour welcomes souls at death, if they have spent their lives in trusting Him, and striven to serve and love Him."   (Francis de Sales)

"I went to sleep: and now I am refreshed –
A strange refreshment: for I feel in me
An inexpressible lightness, and a sense
Of freedom, as I were at length myself,
And ne'er had been before. How still it is:
I hear no more the busy beat of time,
No, nor my fluttering breath, nor struggling pulse,
Nor does one moment differ from the next.
Another marvel: someone has me fast
Within his ample palm: a uniform
And gentle pressure tells me I am not
Self-moving, but borne forward on my way."

Here, through his archetypal Christian, Gerontius, John Henry Newman introduces us to the mysteries which lie beyond the gates of death – mysteries which most of us (if we are honest with ourselves) are loathe to explore. The thought of stepping into the unknown – especially when such a step is final – can prove very daunting, not only because of its irrevocability, but also because we are only too aware of our own failures in attempting to find God, draw close to him, and love him both in himself and in our neighbour. We

114

therefore are inclined to shrink from meeting him from whom no secret is hidden.

On the other hand death is something which the Christian should welcome with open arms because – paradoxically – when we die, we start to live. Now we are only existing, limited by what our bodies are capable of performing, then we shall know even as we are known and, consequently, our lives will become more full and more enriched than is possible whilst we are on this earth.

So it is through the gates of death, and only through those gates, that we can attain that for which we were created – eternal life and everlasting happiness. Moreover this eternal life comes to us from Christ who, by dying destroyed our death and by rising restored our life. St Paul's letter to the Corinthians highlights the fact that it is through Christ that death has been conquered. It is for this reason that when he writes to them, he can mock at death – 'Death, where is your sting? Grave, where is your victory?' (1 Cor 15:55).

As a friend of mine was frequently reminding me before he died, sacred Scripture, describing those things which God has prepared for those who love him, appeals especially to the gourmet! The symbolic picture of Isaiah's banquet, with lots of vintage wines and all good things to eat, foreshadows that vision of heaven in the book of Revelation, where those are happy who are invited to the marriage feast of the Lamb. The companionship and conviviality which a meal affords makes of heaven a pleasing prospect and one which should encourage us in our efforts to reach this goal. Certainly, for those left behind, it gives no cause for mourning. St Teresa of Avila writes: "I do not know how we can grieve for those who go to a place of safety."

But to achieve the Beatific Vision requires constant effort on our part in the different ways I have attempted to explain in previous chapters. To seek to become and to remain close to God in our daily lives on earth, and to resist the many temptations that would lure us away from his service, is of paramount importance and cannot be achieved unaided by the individual. This is particularly important for the Christian to whom much has been given and from whom, therefore, much is expected.

It is greatly to be hoped however that at the Last Judgement, "when the Son of Man comes in his glory, escorted by all the angels" and when he then begins the process of separating men from one another as a shepherd "separates sheep from goats", most of us will be ready. Hopefully then, with the help of God and through our efforts to love him and our neighbour in the ways discussed in previous chapters, we shall then hear Christ say to us,

> "Come, you whom my Father has blessed, take
> for your heritage the kingdom prepared for you
> since the foundation of the world."
>
> (Mt 25:31-33)

Throughout these pages we have considered what it is that might prevent us from recognising Christ as we journey through life along our particular Road to Emmaus. Among other things, we have examined the different ways in which we approach God, the need for us to empty ourselves of notions of self sufficiency, the place of humility and prayer in our lives, the special qualities possessed by the *anawim*, and the role of the Holy Spirit. We have also asked what makes for a genuine Christian community and why, in the context of loving our neighbour and in "breaking bread", we should consider the needs of people in the developing world. Finally we considered how we may separate ourselves from God when we sin and therefore need constant vigilance and possibly even a conversion experience.

Hopefully by taking all these things to heart and acting on them, we could become like the original disciples on the Road to Emmaus, keen to spread the Good News both far and wide, just as they were able to tell others that, "Yes, it is true. The Lord has arisen..."

The Road to Emmaus
(Lk 24:13-35)

That very same day, two of them were on their way to a village called Emmaus, seven miles from Jerusalem, and they were talking together about all that had happened. Now as they talked this over, Jesus himself came up and walked by their side, but something prevented them from recognising him. He said to them, "What matters are you discussing as you walk along?" They stopped short, their faces downcast.

Then one of them, called Cleopas, answered him, "You must be the only person staying in Jerusalem who does not know the things that have been happening there these last few days." "What things?" he asked. "All about Jesus of Nazareth" they answered, "who proved he was a great prophet by the things he said and did in the sight of God and of the whole people; and how our chief priests and our leaders handed him over to be sentenced to death, and had him crucified. Our own hope had been that he would be the one to set Israel free. And this is not all: two whole days have gone by since it all happened; and some women from our group have astounded us: they went to the tomb in the early morning, and when they did not find the body, they came back to tell us they had seen a vision of angels who declared he was alive. Some of our friends went to the tomb and found everything exactly as the women had reported, but of him they saw nothing."

Then he said to them, "You foolish men! So slow

to believe the full message of the prophets! Was it not ordained that the Christ should suffer and so enter into his glory?" Then, starting with Moses and going through all the prophets, he explained to them the passages throughout the Scriptures that were about himself.

When they drew near to the village to which they were going, he made as if to go on; but they pressed him to stay with them. "It is nearly evening" they said, "and the day is almost over." So he went in to stay with them. Now while he was with them at table, he took the bread and said the blessing; then he broke it and handed it to them. And their eyes were opened and they recognised him; but he had vanished from their sight. Then they said to each other, "Did not our hearts burn within us as he talked to us on the road and explained the Scriptures to us?"

They set out that instant and returned to Jerusalem. There they found the Eleven assembled together with their companions, who said to them, "Yes, it is true. The Lord has risen and has appeared to Simon." Then they told their story of what had happened on the road and how they had recognised him at the breaking of bread.

Further Reading

Benedict XVI, *Caritas in Veritate*, 2009.

Jim Forest, *The Ladder of the Beatitudes*, Orbis Books 1999.

Peter France, *Hermits, The Insights of Solitude*, St Martin's Press, 1996.

Albert Gelin, *The Poor of Yahweh*, Liturgical Press, Collegeville, 1964.

Dennis Hamm, *The Beatitudes in Context*, Michael Glazier 1990

James E. Keenan SJ, *Moral Wisdom*, Rowman & Littlefield, 2004.

Jerome Murphy-O'Connor, *Paul His Story*, OUP, 2004.

Henri Nouwen, *Jesus A Gospel,* Orbis 2001.

Ibid, *The Genesee Diary*, Image Books, 1976.

Gerald O'Collins, *The Lord's Prayer*, DLT 2006

Timothy Radcliffe, *Why Go To Church?, The Archbishop of Canterbury's Lent Book,* Continuum, 2008.

Bonnie B. Thurston, *Religious Vows, the Sermon on the Mount and Christian Living*, Liturgical Press, Collegeville 2006.

The Desert Fathers, Sayings of the Early Christian Monks, (Translated and with an Introduction by Benedicta Ward), Penguin, 2003.

The Lives of the Desert Fathers, Introduction by Benedicta Ward, Mowbrays, 1981.

Ed. Ben Quash & Michael Ward, *Heresies and How to Avoid Them*, SPCK 2007

Frances M. Young, *Brokenness and Blessing*, DLT 2007.